90

TRUE CASES FROM THE CID

NICKY MOEY

TIMES BOOKS INTERNATIONAL
Singapore • Kuala Lumpur

Special thanks to Mr Heng Chee How and Ms Veronica Chan from the Republic of Singapore Police Public Relations Department for their invaluable assistance.

All stories in this book are based on actual cases. However, some names and places have been changed to protect the innocent.

Cover photography by Ho Khee Tong.

© **1987 Times Editions Pte Ltd**
© **2000 Times Media Private Limited**
First published in June 1987
Reprinted 1987 (twice), 1988, 1989, 1990, 1991, 1992 (twice), 1994, 1996, 1998, 2000

Published by Times Books International
An imprint of Times Media Private Limited
A member of the Times Publishing Group
Times Centre
1 New Industrial Road
Singapore 536196
Tel: (65) 2848844 Fax: (65) 2854871
E-mail: te@corp.tpl.com.sg
Online bookstore: http://www.timesone.com.sg/te

Times Subang
Lot 46, Subang Hi-Tech Industrial Park
Batu Tiga, 40000 Shah Alam
Selangor Darul Ehsan
Malaysia
Tel & Fax: (603) 7363517
E-mail: cchong@tpg.com.my

Printed in Singapore

ISBN 981 204 204 0

CONTENTS

FOREWORD

With **999: True Cases from the CID**, a co-operative effort between the Republic of Singapore Police and Times Books International, we hope to give our young readers an insight into an aspect of police work often sensationalised on TV and movie screens. Readers of these real-life dramas, however, will not be misled into believing that crimes are solved within a day or a week. Much leg-work, skilful interrogation, investigative know-how and tenacity of purpose go into solving crimes, especially major ones like robbery, kidnapping and murder. Even with such efforts, not all crimes can be solved. Such is the reality of police work, but an unsolved case is 'never closed', and a criminal never safe from retribution.

999: True Cases from the CID – a collection of 11 cases from the CID, written by the young for the young. We hope you will enjoy reading them.

Goh Yong Hong
Commissioner
Republic of Singapore Police
1987

THE FORCE

The Criminal Investigation Department is the elite unit of the Police Force. Men serving in this unit are specially handpicked from the main force according to their performances over the years: they have to be experienced, skilled at conducting investigations and willing to work round the clock and under intense pressure.

The CID is divided into 5 divisions:
1. Major Crimes Division
2. Specialised Crime Division
3. Criminal Intelligence Division
4. Commercial Crime Division
5. Administration Division

The Major Crimes Division itself is made up of
 i. Special Investigation Section (SIS)
 ii. Organised Crime Branch (OCB)
 iii. Interrogation Unit

Special Investigation Section

The branch consists of an officer-in-charge, 6 inspectors and 19 junior officers. 90% of the time, the SIS deals with murders. Other times, it handles kidnappings, major disasters and firearms offences. In 1986, it solved 42 of 66 murders. As for firearms offences, it solved 5 of 14 firearms cases in '86, and the year before, scored 6 out of 6.

Major disasters like the Spyros Fire and the Cable Car Accident were handled by the SIS. When Hotel New World collapsed in March 1986, men from the SIS were there from the beginning to collect information. Later, they helped in the Board of Inquiry – gathering and compiling evidence, coordinating tests on the site and taking down statements of those involved in the hotel's collapse: in 5 months, 10 officers recorded some 500 statements.

Organised Crime Branch

This branch of a strength of 24 takes charge of firearm cases, usually goldsmith and bank robberies in which nobody is killed. Besides that, it investigates rape-cum-robberies and arson committed on government installations and buildings insured for more than $100,000. It also looks into the cases of the Land Division (normal police division); if it detects a pattern in the crimes, or finds that the crimes have something to do with those it is currently investigating, it takes over from the Land Division.

An interesting case which it has solved is about a man who scans the papers for advertisements asking for tenants. Pretending to be a prospective tenant, he'd call the number given, and if he finds the advertiser is a woman, goes to the house or flat to negotiate the price. After some time, he'd tell her he has to leave for a while but would be back. When he returns he'd be carrying some food and drinks, spiked with a sleeping drug. Politely, he'd offer them to the unwitting landlady. And when she falls asleep after consuming them, he'd help himself to the things in the house. After several robberies, the Organised Crime Branch detected his *modus operandi* and arrested him.

Interrogation Unit

A small branch consisting of about 7 officers. Should the SIS or the OCB require their suspects to be questioned over a long period, they enlist the assistance of this unit. Any information elicited from the suspects is then relayed to that particular branch.

Drama at Morningside

THREE SHOT IN HOTEL DRAMA

AUTHOR'S PREFACE TO **HOTEL MORNINGSIDE**

While going through the criminal cases I had been asked to write, I came across this one which I thought was very interesting. The case dealt with a group of policemen who had pursued three vicious criminals all the way from Times House along River Valley Road to Hotel Morningside where the episode ended quite dramatically (If you don't know how it ends, I'll not tell you now, you'll have to read the story). I felt, however, that a third-person narrative would not be as effective as that of a first-person, that is, from the viewpoint of one of the policemen involved; so I asked if I could meet one of the policemen involved, Mohamed Jaynodin bin Soebroto. On 13th September, a Saturday, I had the pleasure of meeting the man himself at the Central Police Station.

Jaynodin is a friendly man, about five-foot four, firmly built, with a standard civil servant haircut. He is reserved, and in the beginning, spoke only to answer certain questions which I asked. Later, when we got to the mainstream of the story, he got more and more excited and talked a good deal and even began to re-enact certain actions in the room. It was very exciting listening to him, almost reliving the incident myself. I found myself leaning forward.

The entire interview lasted a little more than two hours, but like a good night's sleep, it seemed only seconds. I had noted what I wanted and thanked Jaynodin for taking the trouble to meet me.

I have written the story in the first-person, seen through the eyes of Jaynodin.

Here then is Jaynodin's story:

HOTEL MORNINGSIDE

The day was Thursday, September 13th, 1979. At five-thirty in the morning, I got up to go to work. It was still dark then; the morning sun usually doesn't come in till six. My wife and two kids were still sleeping and the only ones awake were my mother and me. We lived at the police headquarters at Onraet Road which is now the Police Academy. It's a congenial place, well situated, a fifteen-minute bus-ride to the main part of town. Nearby was Kampung Nekat, a Malay village, and at the beginning of each new day, we could always hear the cockerel.

I went to have a bath before my morning prayers; I said them every day. There was no heating installation, no shower; I had to use a plastic ladle to scoop water from a large pail. The morning air is cold enough already, and when I splashed the water on myself, I shivered a little, but though it was uncomfortable, the coldness refreshed me a good deal. After the bath, I put on fresh clothes and spent about five to ten minutes praying. Then I left home and took a bus to Orchard Police Station, my workplace. I had been in the force for twelve years already, and in those twelve years, I had made a couple of snatch-thief arrests and chased a couple of housebreakers. The thieves I caught easily. They were ambushed and surrendered without resistance; and for that the force presented me a hundred-dollar cheque. The house-breakers were a different story. It was very dark that night and they sneaked away. But all these incidents were '*kacang*', chicken feed, and never prepared me for this day in September.

It was around seven when I reached the station and I went to the canteen for breakfast. I bought Epok-epok, a Malay curry puff, and a cup of black coffee, and sat alone to eat. I like being alone with my thoughts for company. Whenever I'm away from home and not too occupied with work, I think of my family: what they're doing, whether they were all right, where to take the children out on my off-days, etc.

At seven-thirty, I changed into my uniform and drew arms. My weapon was a 5-chambered .38 Smith and Wesson. Regulars were issued this while national servicemen got the Webley and Scott. Each of us was given ten rounds of ammunition, five to be loaded into the chamber and five to be put in the ammo pouch.

I then went to the briefing room where the supervisor told us our duties for the day. I was assigned to patrol sections 1 and 2, which covered Orchard Road, Clemenceau Avenue, Havelock Road, River Valley Road and Tanglin Road. Two national servicemen accompanied me, SC Cpl Tan Kheng Leong and VC Moorthy Packirisamy. Tan had been with me on one occasion; Moorthy was a new understudy and didn't carry a gun, only a baton.

First, let me tell you something about patrolling. If I'm not wrong, it started way back in '72. We were to cruise around in a car and keep a lookout for suspicious characters, motorcycles to see if they were stolen, accidents, faulty traffic lights that were causing jams, things like that. The routine wasn't new to me, I had even patrolled the assigned area several times.

We left the station at eight. I drove. Tan took the seat next to me and Moorthy the back. As usual, we kept our eyes peeled for anything that demanded our attention. We spoke little, and when we did it was about making a good arrest that day. By about ten we found nothing unusual. I drove to Zion Road where two guys were to take over the car while we were to go on foot patrol. It was a kind of exchange: we patrolled on foot while they took the vehicle. After an hour, they'd come back and we'd take over again. I don't know the real name of the guy who took my place as driver. Folks called him McGarrett, and I called him McGarrett too. The other guy was Suppiah. They took the car and we, Tan, Moorthy and I, took a walk around an HDB estate, which turned out to be a pleasant, undisturbed one.

Around eleven, McGarrett picked us up and dropped us back at the police station for lunch. Earlier, I had bought a packet of Nasi Biryani and I went to the canteen to eat. When I had finished, there was more than half an hour to spare before McGarrett came back so I went to the rest room to read the papers and rest a little.

McGarrett came back at twelve. Tan, Moorthy and I got into the car.

The sun had climbed up to the middle of the sky and was baking the ground and heating the air around us. As we drove along, we received a walkie talkie call asking us to head for Nan Chiau Girls' School at Kim Yam Road. Nothing really serious happened: an eleven- to twelve-year-old girl had injured her knee. I asked her if she would like to be taken to hospital and she said she would. We called for an ambulance and while waiting, we took down the girl's particulars.

Shortly, the ambulance arrived, took the girl away and we continued on our rounds.

I came out of Kim Yam Road into River Valley Road, cruising real slow. Tan was recording the girl's injury on the log sheet. And then as I approached Times House, I saw them – three men walking towards Times House. Something about the way they walked gave me an uneasy sensation, what we police call a hunch. I said to my buddies, 'Those three fellows don't look right.'

Tan said, 'Let's check them out.'

I sounded the horn and when they turned around to look at us I pointed at them and then pointed at the sidewalk. For a few seconds they stood very still, and I could see panic swelling on their faces. They dashed across the road. All three wore slippers and they ran a bit awkwardly and one of them left a slipper on the road.

I did a quick semi-circle, bringing the car to the opposite lane. The three of us were out the moment I jammed on the brakes. The suspects were less than six feet away. They began scuttling up a low hill. We scuttled up the hill too. I wasn't feeling too well because it was hot and I was sweating and the Nasi Biryani I had for lunch was tossing about in my stomach.

On top of the hill, we came upon a barren piece of ground. Beyond that were some bushes. I saw what was behind the bushes and almost grinned.

It was a fence. And I thought, That's it boys; war's over.

The idiots were still running. I was tense with excitement but I wasn't scared. These boys don't look dangerous, I told myself; can '*makan*' them quite easily.

We went for them, one to one. The one I was after was a short fellow. As he came to the fence he fell forward. I pulled him up by the back of his shirt. No problem at all. My buddies got their men without much sweat too. These boys seemed docile enough.

We sort of herded them together and stood around them. The action was over and I was cooling down, the excitement in me ebbing, my pulse slowing to normal.

'See if they're carrying anything unusual,' I said to Moorthy and he began to body-search them.

I don't know how, but there is Moorthy slapping them from head to foot trying to find a hidden weapon or something and here stand Kheng Leong and I, watching them like vultures, and right in front of our noses this guy yells loudly in Hokkien and before his yell could trail off into the air he and the short fellow have knives in their hands. The shouter then pulled out Moorthy's truncheon, quick and easy.

I'll say this for them: they were quick on the draw all right.

The third fellow didn't carry a knife, but the two who had raised them up to striking position. Their eyes glared with an unexpected ferocity, especially the one who had shouted and taken Moorthy's baton. He was tall, skinny, savage-looking. Later Tan told me that what he shouted was, 'Fight to the last! Either they die or we die!'

The short guy with the knife suddenly attacked Tan. Tan shouted for me and I ran over. The attacker changed his mind and sprang away.

We drew our revolvers.

Now you might think that it's a piece of cake when you have guns against knives; we were out of striking range of the knives and I could have simply squeezed the trigger and let Smith and Wesson make my day. But I wasn't called Harry and this wasn't the movies we're talking about. You might ask me why I couldn't have aimed at the legs or somewhere non-lethal. Answer: none of us had opened fire at another human being before, it was strange even to think about it. And we were officers of the law, supposed to use our weapons only if it was absolutely necessary, only if lives were threatened. It wouldn't be too fair to shoot a couple of guys who were just standing with knives in their hands.

'Drop the knives!' I shouted at them. 'Drop them!'

They didn't. All they did was take a few steps backwards, slowly, knives still raised. We moved a step forward for every step they took backwards, keeping our relative distance fixed. The stalemate went on till they reached the edge of the crest. Then turning, they ran down the slope.

We followed them down. Once in a while, one of us shouted, 'Stop! Stop! Put your weapons down!' but they just kept running.

They were a little ahead of us and at the bottom of the hill, I saw them going for our patrol car. One wanted to start the engine but what he wanted to find was jingling in my pocket. When they found the key wasn't there they hurried across River Valley Road. Traffic along the road was heavy then, the people who stared curiously from their cars just went on staring till their vehicles disappeared out of sight.

On the other side of the road, the three men saw us catching up with them. They made a surprise turn-around and came towards us. Skinny headed for me, his face aggressive, snarling with hate. My eyes were trained on him alone; I didn't know what was happening to my buddies, or his, for it suddenly seemed like there were only two of us left in the world, foe confronting foe in a fight to the death.

Smith and Wesson was in my hand and I fired. The gun went off and he was still running towards me!

I shrank back, thinking that the damn gun had played me out. Then I realised it could also be that I had missed. But there wasn't time for a second shot. Skinny had come within range, his dagger raised like a cobra ready to strike. And it suddenly occurred to me that this wasn't a game, that the knife wasn't plastic, that I couldn't raise two fingers and say, 'Peace! peace! peace!' and he'd stop. We weren't playing police and thief. We WERE police and thief. I could possibly be hurt, killed.

The knife came swooping down. I dodged, my heart pumping crazily, hoping it wouldn't hit me.

It didn't.

'Throw down the knife!' I shouted, more to allay my fears than anything, expecting another onslaught, but he retreated and started running again. His friends joined him.

I looked at my buddies and they looked all right. We ran after them.

The six of us tore down the road, trees and traffic flew past us. As we turned right into Jalan Kuala, two men with knives jumped us from the bushes. Skinny sprang at me. I squeezed the trigger twice, instinctively. There had been no time to aim and the bullets whined off somewhere. Then I called out to Tan to fire, too. I heard the explosion from Tan's Webley but I didn't know if he had hit his target.

We reached a crowded bus-stop, and I thought help was at hand, but the people only stared facelessly at us, not doing anything else, and I wondered why.

Next to the bus-stop was a taxi-stand. A taxi was stationed there. Skinny went up to it. He tried the door. It was locked. He then pushed the knife in the narrow space that the incompletely wound up screen had left, trying to force the screen down. The taxi driver leaned over, worked at the handle frantically and the screen went up.

They abandoned the idea of getting into the cab and ran straight ahead. We kept close.

During the chase I looked back once and found that only Tan was with me. Moorthy had somehow disappeared. I didn't know what had happened to him. All I cared about was getting those thugs.

I saw them come upon a junction. Straight ahead was another crowded spot, so they veered right, in the direction of Hotel Morningside. There was something about the way they fled that bothered me; I couldn't help getting the feeling that they could have, without much effort, widened the gap between us; and if they tried hard enough, lose us, but they had chosen to slow down, as if – as if they WANTED a fight! They wanted to kill us! A couple of times, Skinny spun around and tried attacking me. I fired, aiming at the legs, intending to wound him so it'd be easy to take him in. But he was moving and I was moving and the shots went wild.

At Hotel Morningside, they ran past an archway which had the sign, Seafood Satay Garden. There was an old man, a Malay, about – I don't know – maybe fifty to sixty years old tiredly sweeping the cement floor, unaware of the men. Skinny came up to the back of him, locked an arm at his neck and pulled him backwards, using the old man as a shield.

'Release the man!' I shouted as I ran.

Suddenly I felt nervous, desperate, unsure of myself. I had failed to prevent them from escaping on top of the hill, now they had an extra leverage.

I didn't know how it could happen so fast. I had caught up with them and was standing a few feet away from Skinny who had the gardener in an arm-lock, thinking how I could handle the situation when Shortie ran around Skinny and towards me. The blade in his hand flashed, fast. My quickest reaction was to hold up my hand to protect myself.

The next thing I saw was blood trickling down a cut between my second and third finger. I didn't like the sight of my own blood. A sudden rage exploded in me. The punk was at point blank range and I was going to let him have it.

I pulled the trigger.

The hammer clicked harmlessly.

Shortie didn't know my revolver was empty and instead of attacking the second time, he sprang back to avoid a shot. The three men with the hostage moved into a Chinese restaurant, which was much like any other: papered walls, round tables under white sheets, chairs with cushion seats, glasses of Chinese tea.

The lunchtime crowd was still having a feast. Everyone stared at us when we made our entrance. I had expected someone to help us, but nobody came forward; they preferred remaining safe at their tables. Tan and I yelled a few 'Release the man!' between us, knowing that we should have saved our breaths. They were several feet away and I then turned to Tan and whispered, 'My gun's empty. Go after them first.'

The men dragged the gardener across the hall, out to an open space beyond. I was worried for Tan, he was only a national serviceman. Leaving him alone with those gangsters was the last thing I wished. I hastily dug into my ammo pouch, grabbed once and came up with three rounds, snapped open the cylinder, pushed the bullets in, snapped it shut, and sprinted after my buddy. I would have loaded all five into the cylinder, but there wasn't time. When I came out into the open, I found myself at a car-park. They were standing there waiting for me. Again I couldn't help getting the feeling that, somehow knowing I was the leader, they wanted to dispatch me first, then take care of Tan, who was having his revolver trained at them.

I looked at Skinny and Skinny looked at me. He was standing at the back of the gardener, one arm around the gardener's neck. His other hand held the knife. Quite suddenly, he stabbed inwards, planting the knife slightly below the gardener's chest; then he ploughed the knife downwards, cutting deep.

That was a mean, cruel trick, meant to shake me up, confuse me so he could make his attack. And it worked. An instant later he leapt towards me. The blade came down. It caught me in the left shoulder. Pain streaked across my entire arm.

The gun was now my only chance to stop him. He was ready to stab me again and this time it might not be only my arm. I squeezed the trigger, and as I did so I suddenly realised to my horror that in the restaurant, I had not looked when I reloaded my gun. If I had loaded the three rounds in the wrong chambers the gun would go click on the first squeeze, and that precious fraction of a second could give Skinny enough time to stab me.

Smith and Wesson roared. And I saw Skinny suddenly standing very straight. He remained so for several seconds, his eyes closed, white froth creaming over his mouth. Then he pitched forward and fell on his face.

When I fired, I heard Tan's Webley go off too. And now, all three men lay prone on the ground. I walked carefully up to Skinny and pressed the barrel of the revolver against his head, not knowing then

The aftermath. The man, being examined by an ambulance attendant, died shortly after this picture was taken.

that he was dead, and that my revolver was empty. My left arm had been bleeding badly, and the strain of all the excitement and all the running caught up on me. I felt weak, dizzy. Far off, I heard the siren of an approaching police car, and I knew Moorthy had left us to call for help. The dizziness was getting to me and the sound of the siren grew weaker and weaker until there was nothing.

I awoke to find myself in an ambulance. Next to me was the old gardener. He was alive. And I was alive. Much later, I learnt that I had fired all three rounds at one go. One hit Skinny at the left upper arm, another his left thigh, and the fatal one had entered sideways through the top of his right shoulder, burrowed through about eighteen inches of his body, and emerged just under his left shoulder. Shortie was shot in the right arm and somewhere in the waist, but he survived. The third guy was unhurt.

I had to undergo therapy sessions at the Singapore General Hospital three times a week to get my arm and fingers working again.

The force promoted me to the rank of corporal and I now work in an office from eight to five because my injury wouldn't let me do duties outdoors. But whenever I think of that day, the thirteenth day of the ninth month of the year nineteen seventy nine, I always tell myself that I'm very, very lucky to be alive.

* * * * * * * * * * * * * *

WHEN LOVE DIES

Lim Keehock and Jenny Lee met under the most likely circumstance: he was a teacher from a night school and she came into his life as a student. Keehock was almost fifty, skinny, with a sunken face and a high forehead. Jenny was thirty-nine years old, slim, and in spite of her age, retained her youthful beauty which must have captivated Keehock the moment they met. He decided then that he would be denying himself an excellent opportunity for love if he didn't woo her. So woo her he did. And to his delight, his comely student began to respond to his overtures, a little at first, showing the little signs a courted woman is very apt at showing, then more profusely.

Love blossomed. And if not for one factor theirs would be as fine, happy and contented a love as one could wish. They were both married.

Jenny had been married for ten years. She lived with her husband, a carpenter and daughter at their Bukit Batok flat. Her daughter Mei Lian was ten years old, and people who knew them always said that she took after her mother.

Keehock had two teenage daughters and a wife who was suffering from a liver disease. But he seldom spent time with them, and they never missed him. Even before he met Jenny, his family had suspected him of having other affairs, for he often came home late, not telling anyone where he had been or what he had been doing.

The two saw each other often; she on the pretext of wanting extra tuition and he on that of tutoring her. Besides that, they spoke on the phone, secretly.

Jenny's husband eventually suspected something, and before long, made the discovery. He confronted the lover one day and told the latter to cease all communications with his wife. Keehock agreed, not without an apology. It would be wrong to carry on. There would be no more calls and lessons for Jenny.

That, of course, was a lie. The lovers met clandestinely this time, and whether or not her husband knew is a matter of conjecture. Even if he did know, there wasn't much he could do, for he loved her too.

A year later, Jenny's husband died in an automobile accident, which was a tragedy and a boon to her. It was all right now to be seen in public with her former teacher.

She invited Keehock to her house often, and in time, he came of his own accord, helping himself to the food and comfort she offered. Occasionally, he slept at her place. The hospitality was reciprocated. He brought her and Mei Lian to his flat at Woodlands, introducing her to his family as a student of his. His family members treated her cordially, though not without reserve. And she too, began to go there uninvited. The friendliness his wife and daughters accorded her initially soon began to fade; they couldn't help feeling that she was not only impinging upon their lives, but also conducting Keehock's love away from them.

All this went on for some time, a married man loving a pretty widow, careless of the hurt and embarrassment and shame he was causing his wife and children.

According to Jenny's mother-in-law, Jenny once had an affair with another teacher before she met Keehock. Her husband had caught them together at a playground and, after some exchange of words, managed to break up the affair. That was five years ago. And when Jenny wanted to take up lessons again, her husband insisted that she study under a new teacher, who turned out to be Keehock. And she had fallen for him, too.

One thing Jenny didn't know about her lover was that he had her qualities. Which was why he had fallen for her in the first place, and which was to be the turning point of their relationship.

There are always the tell-tale signs which a closely related companion can detect, however much the other party tries to conceal: a slip of the tongue, a gesture, an expression; and somehow, Jenny suspected that Keehock was keeping, besides a wife and herself, a third woman. She fell out of her head-long infatuation with him. And when they spoke on the phone that night, she let drop her decision.

'That's how it is,' she said. 'I don't want to have anything to do with you any more.'

'I don't know what you're saying,' he remonstrated. 'There isn't any other woman!'

'I don't want you to call me any more,' she remained steadfast. 'And don't come to my place again.'

But he wanted to see her again. Despite having had affairs with other women, Keehock must have still loved her very much, and wasn't willing to let her walk out of his life. He called her again and again, denying the existence of any third woman and explaining himself to her. When that didn't work he became irritated, determinedly vengeful. A few days after she announced the end of their affair, Jenny heard a bottle explode into fragments against her door.

She became frightened.

The incident was repeated twice. He was not afraid of making a fool of himself before her neighbours, because he knew he was also making a fool of her. Standing outside her door, he'd hurl loud, abusive language at her, maliciously exposing all the skeletons for everyone to hear, threatening her and Mei Lian.

His plan worked. To keep the neighbours from peeking at them, to stop Keehock from hollering in public, to save herself the trouble, the embarrassment, Jenny made the mistake of her life. She let him in.

Far from welcoming him, she only allowed him in because it was the only way in which to keep him quiet. He would sit around, or watch television, or have a drink while she went about her own work.

Love died. At least Jenny's did. She no longer enjoyed his company, but he still insisted on visiting her, lolling in her flat, sleeping there at times; he had warned her that he was prepared to give them a lot of trouble if she refused him entry. She reported him to the police, but was told that it was a civil matter, that she had to take up summon actions against him, and she didn't know how. She then tried speaking to his wife, asking for help in persuading him not to trouble her any longer. But Keehock's wife couldn't do much: she was having enough trouble with her liver condition, let alone an unfaithful husband.

Jenny was resigned.

It was a night in November. At ten-thirty Keehock appeared at her flat. He smelled of stout. There was no doubt he was going to stay for the night. Jenny didn't want another scene and opened the door for him.

The three slept in the same room. Jenny and her daughter Mei Lian slept in the master bed. He slept at the rear.

It was all right, Jenny told herself. He'd sleep it off and be gone by morning.

Around five in the morning, Keehock awoke. He looked at Jenny and saw she was asleep. His eyes fell on Mei Lian. She was sleeping in her pyjamas. She seemed pleasant and attractive, even at her age. An urge stirred in him, not a tremendous one, but something like a glowing cinder. He kept looking at the child, letting the urge expand. If only he could touch her, he thought. What did a young girl feel like anyway? He looked at Jenny again: her eyes were closed. Then he looked back at the child: she was asleep. They wouldn't know. And what they didn't know wouldn't hurt them. There would be no harm if he did it. Just once.

He crawled out of his corner, quietly, and moved towards the girl on the bed. His hand stretched out –

'What are you doing!' he heard Jenny cry. The hand withdrew.

'I . . .' he whimpered.

'You touched her!' she hissed at him.

'I'm sorry, Jenny,' he said. 'I couldn't help myself. Please forgive me. I'll never do it again.'

'Get out!' she said. 'Get out of my house now!'

He walked down the street in the cold, deserted morning. The rest of the day, he remained out, but at 9.00 that night, he returned, intending to stay there again for the night. Fifty minutes later, police officers came and arrested him on the charge of child-molest. He was brought to Joo Chiat Police Station where he admitted to the charge, then released on bail for the night. The next day he claimed trial which was fixed for mention in late December; until then, he was to be remanded in Queenstown Prison.

Keehock's family bailed him out. The amount was $5,000. He seemed a changed man after that: he stayed home often, the quarrelling between husband and wife ceased; and he was attentive to his family's needs and began to show a lot of care. And what he finally did six days later came as a shock to everyone.

That day, at nine in the morning, he left his house without telling anyone where he was going. At two-thirty in the afternoon, as Jenny was leaving her study-centre for home, he came up to her.

'I left some things in your place,' he said. 'I want to collect them now.'

She eyed him with suspicion. Somehow, he did not appear or sound right. She went to the nearest phone and called her mother-in-law to ask for advice.

'Be careful,' the old woman told her. 'I wouldn't trust him if I were you. Don't forget he has threatened to kill you and your family before.'

But it wasn't any use. Despite Jenny's remonstrations, Keehock managed to get into her flat.

Chan Geok Leng, living a few metres away, was watching television with her sisters when she heard another neighbour at the window calling for help. They opened the door and the neighbour said excitedly, 'There's trouble in Jenny's house.' No sooner had the words been spoken than they heard a woman's voice screaming for help, and Geok Leng recognised it as Jenny's. A moment later, they saw Jenny rushing out, her T-shirt soaked with blood. Jenny ran into her flat, and as she entered, collapsed. Geok Leng's mother, using cotton, cloth and towels, tried to stop the bleeding. Geok Leng noticed that the woman in pain was reaching for a phone, and, assuming that she wanted to call the police, dialled the number for her.

Ambulance attendants came into the hall. They began to revive the bleeding woman. The people watched, worriedly.

After a time, the attendant said, 'She's dead.'

Police went into Jenny's house and found him in a crouching position on the floor. The yellow tiles were streaked with red. A chisel lay on the floor beside him. There were stab wounds all over his body and neck. He, too, was dead.

Investigations and a *post mortem* showed that

Keehock had stabbed his lover first, then painfully committed suicide.

****

MANHUNT

Victoria Theatre and Victoria Memorial Hall stand together at Empress Place, the heart of the city, between the shopping paradise of Orchard Road and the business and law offices of Shenton Way. Next to them is the Parliament House, and a little farther down, the Supreme Court and City Hall.

Eileen Tan, account assistant with Dominick and Co., had been with the company for four months. Her job required her to withdraw money from the company's bank to pay the rest of the employees at the end of each month.

On 30th March 1984, at a little after eleven in the morning, Eileen, accompanied by colleagues Ng Ming Ming and Jacqueline De Souza, arrived at DBS at Battery Road to collect money for the company's staff. An overdraft of $10,016/- had been arranged to be withdrawn, and when she received the cash, she put it in a brown envelope. DBS had given her the money in nine $500/- bills and other smaller denominations, and she decided to go to another bank to have those large bills changed into smaller ones so it would be more convenient to pay the staff in their company. The three of them set off towards the Post Office Savings Bank at Empress Place. Finding that bank too crowded, they walked over to UOB at the Victoria Memorial Hall to exchange the bills. After getting the smaller denominations, they made towards Ming Ming's car parked at North Boat Quay, behind the theatre, Eileen with the envelope tucked under her arm.

As they passed under the porch of Victoria Theatre, she felt a sudden tug at her envelope from behind. She spun around and saw a Chinese man, about five-foot five, the envelope of money in his hand. She reached out to snatch the envelope back. She had managed to catch hold of the edge of the envelope when she heard a bang, then came a searing pain at the right side of her neck. Her legs lost their strength and she sat down on the ground. Her two friends turned and saw a man running towards a motorcycle where an accomplice waited. He wore a light coloured crash helmet and was dressed in a white shirt and brown pants. In his left hand was the envelope, and in his right, a piece of steel resembling a gun. He mounted the back of the motorcycle which then roared off. A Caucasian tourist taking photographs of the city saw them fleeing and photographed them. Another witness to the theft managed to take down the motorcycle number, AQ 3128.

Eileen, on the floor, began to feel dizzy; she could see people crowding around. Someone came to attend to her. She had an entry wound on the outer side of her neck and an exit wound in the middle. She was brought to the hospital, warded and discharged

Timely photograph taken by a passing Caucasian tourist, of the robbers' hasty getaway on their motorcycle, AQ 3128.

two days later, her 5-month-old pregnancy un-affected. In point of fact, two shots had been fired: at the scene of the crime, police discovered two bullet casings: one at the entrance of the porch and the other on a pavement in front of Victoria Theatre. But only one bullet was found. It had hit a door beam, ricocheted off the porch ceiling, and landed on the tiled floor.

Investigations were conducted, but for nearly four months, neither the thief nor his accomplice could be traced. Then on the afternoon of 30th July, the break came.

Inspector Gan Kim Tian had just collected a copy of a marriage certificate at UIC Building, Shenton Way. He came out of the building and walked along the pedestrian pavement. Across the street two men were loitering before a DBS Bank. The taller man was in blue T-shirt and the other in striped black short sleeves. Gan spotted them and didn't like the way they were behaving. As he watched, a suspicion grew. After ten minutes, he crossed the road towards the bank for a closer look, and saw that the shorter man wore a gold watch and the taller one a silver strapped watch. In a flash of memory, he remembered the photograph of the two men on the bike taken by the tourist the day Eileen Tan was robbed: one had worn a gold watch and the other a silver one.

He scanned the area for a pay-phone for he knew he couldn't arrest the two men alone. There were none in sight, so he rushed back to his office to summon help. At the ops room, he called Inspector Michael Chan, related what he had seen. Michael came down with five men.

Back at Shenton Way, the two men were getting on the Yamaha 125 when the lawmen arrived. The rider put on a black helmet and the pillion rider a LIGHT COLOURED helmet.

Gan took down the number, FA 3981C, returned to office, checked with the Criminal Record Office and found that the number belonged to a Kawasaki 125 which had been stolen from Ang Mo Kio.

He instructed D/Cpl Quek and D/Sgt Lim to return to Shenton Way to keep watch. He then called the OC and explained his suspicion, giving him the number of the bike.

One and a half hours later, at 2.15 p.m., D/Cpl Quek called.

'We're at Shenton Way, near Golden Bridge,' Quek said. 'We've spotted the motorcycle. It's now parked behind a lorry in front of ICB Building.'

'Keep watching,' Gan told them. In ten minutes, he was with Quek.

'The motorcycle's left already,' Quek said. 'It's not gone far away.'

Together with twelve detectives, Gan and Quek combed the area; the motorcycle and the rider were spotted by them in front of DBS.

'Keong, Chan,' Gan instructed. 'Make the arrest. The rest of you, look out for the accomplice.'

There was barely a struggle as the detectives apprehended their man, but the arrest had attracted a crowd, and Gan decided to hand the captive back to CID so that it would not attract the attention of his accomplice. 'Cpl Quek,' he said, 'you and Sgt Lim continue searching. I'm bringing the suspect back for questioning.'

The two detectives eventually found their man, only before they could arrest him, he whipped out a pistol and fired at them. The detectives drew their revolvers, fast. Lawmen and outlaw traded shots. Then the gunman clambered onto a lorry and fled.

When Inspector Gan returned to Shenton Way half an hour later, the sergeant told him what had happened, and that Cpl Quek had gone after the man. Gan called DO Radio, asked him to inform all divisions to keep a lookout for a gunman who could have been shot.

The answer from the DO came: a male Chinese was lying in a lorry at Teo Hong Road. They drove to the place and found the lorry, the driver slumped against the steering wheel. He had been shot dead.

The gunman, suspected to be the one who had robbed Eileen Tan four months ago, had escaped. There was one thing left to do.

Back at the CID office, Inspectors Gan, Michael Chan, and several others interrogated the accused, Lim Woo Sung. He denied involvement in any robbery.

'What is the name of your accomplice?'

'I don't know.'

'What is the name of your accomplice?'

'I told you I don't know.'

'What is the name of your accomplice?'

'I call him Ah Chai.'

'What do you know about him?'

'I don't know.'

The accused was shown the photograph, taken by the tourist, of two men escaping on a motorcycle. 'Were you the rider of the bike?'

'No. Kao Hei – he could be the rider.'

'I'll ask you again. What do you know about Ah Chai?'

'I said I don't know. He only told me to meet him at Shenton Way.'

At 1800 hrs, an anonymous call informed the police that the gunman was hiding at Blk 2 of Jalan Batu. The detectives headed for the scene. They found nothing.

They returned to headquarters and continued interrogating the accused, who still insisted he knew nothing.

Other anonymous calls came that sent the lawmen on chases that lasted from that same night till the next morning. They raided a vacant house at Bukit Pasoh Road, and another at North Bridge Road. At Pearl's Hill Terrace, blood stains were seen inside and outside a lift, so some officers guarded the ground floor while others did a house to house search; and finally at Blk 44, Toa Payoh.

The gunman wasn't even seen.

Five ten in the morning. The men returned to CID where they attended a briefing by OC Organised Crime Branch. They were to raid a flat in Blk 66, Circuit Road – probably given by Lim who had to tell them where he sometimes went to – with Inspector Seah and a party of officers, and try to locate articles that could connect this case to the Empress Place Robbery. And if they could locate Ah Chai's telephone number, the better.

The occupant of the flat turned out to be none other than Lim's mistress. They found a piece of paper with two telephone numbers written on it. The mistress said that lately, Lim had been associating with a man who picked Lim up every day in a white car (5745). The mistress returned to CID with them and was interviewed by an officer.

As for Lim Woo Sung, at 0715 hrs, after 15 hours of intensive grilling, the tightly-shut clamp finally yielded. He gave the name of his accomplice. Police are withholding his name, so we shall call him X. The car he drove was ET 5745.

Police ran a check on the two telephone numbers and the car number. One of the numbers was traced to a house in Tanjong Katong Road, and the other to a flat at Prince Charles Square. The car licence plate was traced to a woman who lived in that same flat at Prince Charles Square. That same day, police seized the car.

The next afternoon, at 4.58 p.m., 2nd August '84, two days after Lim had been arrested, police set an ambush once again at Pearl's Hill Terrace for Kao Hei, whom Lim had named as the rider of the motorcycle at the Empress Place Robbery.

The wait of one and a half hours paid off. Their man turned up and was arrested. His real name: Eu Kim Chuan. Eu, at the CID office, admitted he was that rider in the robbery at Empress Place. And the one who had robbed Eileen Tan and shot her, the one who tried robbing DBS bank with Lim, who escaped in a lorry and killed the driver in cold blood, was X.

Subsequently, from the confessions of the two accused, eight other people were arrested. From them, police found out that a good number of robberies (more than 12) had been committed by X and each of them.

Eu first met X at a brothel in Geylang four years ago; although he had invited X to his wedding dinner in 1981, Eu did not meet up with him again until February 1983.

He was having some porridge at a Geylang market when X came up to him.

'I'm in debt,' X told him. 'I owe Ah Long (illegal moneylender) money, I have about $500/- tontine money to pay up, I lost quite a lot at the races. My partner has stopped joining me in snatch thefts because we had a quarrel.' Then he asked Eu, 'You have a class 2 licence, right? Why don't you join me? We can do a good job together.'

Eu was undecided. 'I don't know. I've never committed a crime before. I don't even know how to commit a snatch theft. No, I don't think I want this.'

But X pleaded. 'Please, help me. I'm in debt. Just a few robberies will do. I'm not asking you to do the stealing, all you do is to take me to the target area. I'll do the robbing, then we scoot off together.'

'I don't know,' Eu said. 'I'll consider it.'

About a week after the incident, X called Eu at his home.

'How about it?' he asked Eu.

'I'm not sure,' Eu answered. 'I don't think I should do it.' Yet, perhaps unconsciously, his resistance was eroding, slowly.

Five days passed, and X called to ask him again. He was persistent.

'Call me back after Chinese New Year,' Eu told him. 'I'll need time to think about it.'

X took his word for it. A fortnight after Chinese New Year, he called Eu again.

'Well,' he asked. 'Have you decided? I've also got Kwan to join me.'

'Okay, okay,' Eu said, hesitantly.

'Good. I have already got a stolen motorcycle for you to ride. Stay at home and wait for my call,' X said.

On 19th July '83, the two men collaborated. At Lorong 3, Geylang, they waited till a woman appeared. Eu waited with his motorcycle engine running while X went to do the job. In a moment, X came running back. He jumped on the motorcycle and told Eu to ride off quickly.

X had promised Eu 30 per cent of the loot. When they met again at a coffee shop at Jalan Sultan, X gave Eu a sum of $3,000/-. Two days later, Eu learnt from the Chinese papers that the total amount of money stolen from the woman was about $40,000/-. The robber, Eu read, had been armed with a gun.

With money coming in so easily, it became hard for Eu to turn down other 'assignments'.

1st August, 1983. The two men attempted to rob an old man at the DBS basement car-park. The old man refused to surrender the money and X shot at him.

30th March '84. They decided to rob another woman who would be carrying her company payroll out of DBS bank; this was Eileen Tan. Prior to this, Eu learnt that X had lost money at the races again. X called him the night before the robbery and asked if he'd like another 'job'.

'All right,' Eu said.

'Pick up the stolen motorcycle from the back of Textile Centre at ten tomorrow morning,' X said.

At ten the next day, Eu reached Textile Centre and saw X already waiting. The two of them were to go separately and meet at Chartered Bank, Battery Road. Eu rode the motorcycle there while X went in a car. He reached Battery Road in twenty minutes and parked the motorcycle on a pavement near a fountain. In a distance, he saw Kwan, X's other partner who was supposed to watch the woman. Eu nodded at him. X arrived twenty minutes later, parking his car at the basement of Raffles Square. He got out of the car, walked over to Kwan, talked to him. Kwan then started walking into DBS. X remained where he was. Eu stood next to the stolen motorcycle. In half an hour, Kwan emerged from the bank and passed a message to X. X, after listening, came over to Eu.

'I want you to ride the bike to Empress Place, in front of Victoria Memorial Hall. The "target" is already there.'

Eu obeyed. He parked the motorcycle and waited again. Half an hour later, he spotted X standing at the porch entrance of Victoria Memorial Hall. X signalled to him, telling him to get ready. The woman and her friends came out a moment later, walking towards North Boat Quay. She had a brown envelope tucked under her arm. Eu started the engine and climbed on the vehicle. X put on his light coloured helmet and started stealing up towards the women whose backs were turned to him.

Seconds after, Eu heard two reports, one following the other. In his rear-view mirror, he saw X sprinting towards him. He felt the suspension compressed as X jumped on the back seat. Hurriedly, he sped off towards Textile Centre, Jalan Sultan. From there, the two separated. That night, Eu received a call from X. The next day, X gave Eu $1,000/- for his part in the theft, telling Eu that he needed the money and would pay him the rest of his share later.

Before Eu's arrest at Pearl's Hill Terrace, he and X committed yet another robbery at Realty Centre, making off with $30,000/- of which Eu received $3,000/-.

Kwan, the third accomplice, was arrested by the CID on 3rd August, 1984, less than six hours after Eu.

The instigator of all these robberies, the one who has no qualms about shooting anyone, killing anyone, X, is still at large. This man is dangerous. His robberies are always carefully planned. He never works alone. When he strikes, there is always someone waiting close by with a runaway vehicle. He solicits help by offering a percentage of the loot, then giving less than agreed. He obtains accurate information on when and where a payroll is taking place and watches his victims carefully before striking. And he is always ready to use his gun, again.

LUCRE

Mr Runme Shaw glanced with a nagging unease at the small, white envelope before him. It was just like any other ordinary letter, addressed to him, the postal date 15 Mar 1976 stamped on it. But something about it didn't look right. Something was odd. It was typed. That was it, that was what's wrong. Typed letters meant business letters, and letters involving business usually had the company trademark printed on the envelope. This one didn't.

He picked it up and ripped off the entire length of the top, tearing the stamp away. The letter was light blue, thin, and folded three times. Like the envelope, it was type-written. Shaw unfolded the paper and read.

Dear Sir,

We like to introduce our self, we are from an "Intention Party" our party is inneed of a supporter, we decided to choose you, hape you would kindly support us with the sum of two handred thousand (200,ooo /=).

remember your family and property will be burn down or dead. if any mistake we are confident that in this case, you were to report to the police of using trap. Nither false will use sure thing is not a threaten to us, we are not same as other secret society in singapore, We believe police will be inform . the difference between the "Intention Party" and other secret society is that we plan to sacrifice our member if we need too... .

The rest of the letter warned Shaw to take it seriously and to await further instructions. It ended with: Thank You!

From
Intention Party

15-3-76

Three Chinese characters which were the translation of 'Intention Party' were written on the right of the words. A German swastika with a skull at the centre was drawn below the date.

Shaw re-read the letter, frowning. There were a few possibilities: The letter might just turn out to be a prank, a cruel joke by an adversary who meant only to scare him, in which case there was really nothing to worry about. Or that the threat could be real, meaning he had to pay for the safety of his property and the lives of his family members. But giving in to them would only encourage further extortion, which, in time, could bleed a multi-millionaire like him dry. There was only one alternative. At four-forty that same afternoon, Supt SS Au-Yong Weng Wah handed the letter to ASP Tan Ngo Chew in the presence of Shaw's bodyguard, Loh Poh Cheng. The ASP read the letter, then accompanied the bodyguard to Shaw's office for Shaw to make an official report. Tan sent the letter to the lab to have fingerprints lifted. The lab boys found none. He also had his phone number changed and unlisted in case they tried to contact him, hoping feebly that failing to do so, they might withdraw their threats. A mobile patrol was to conduct constant visits to Queen Astrid Park.

Six days later, two identical letters were sent to him, one to his home at Queen Astrid Park and the other to his office at Robinson Road. Again, they were sent in small, white envelopes; blue letter paper, type-written, and dated 22nd March 1976:

Dear Sir.

We are the "Intention Party". we want to ransom from you $2000,000. on the 15th of March we have already send you a letter to your home and ring you up several time. we got no reply from you, Now we will send you two more letters, one to your office and the other to your home. It within 3 days time we still get no reply first we will burn down your theater, secondly we will have your family lives death. informing of police is not a theater to us, we Intention party rather die then to be poor. Now prepare $200,000. half in one hundred note and the other half is fifty dollars note. All in old note and not according to numbers wrap up in newspaper and putin a black plastice bag, the one who send the money must be in red shirt and pants get every thing prepare and wait for our phone. We will contact you when you receive our letter.

Remember to kill your family is not a easy thing but to burn down your theater is a simple job.

Thank You!

"INTENTION PARTY"

This time, there was no doubt about it. These people meant business. But there was nothing Shaw nor the police could do. The letters could have been sent by anyone. The question now was: when would they strike? And where?

25th March 1976. The offices of Shaw Centre were closed. Manuel Enock of Hansen Security Agency and security officer for the night looked at his watch. 10.00 p.m. He stifled a yawn. It was quiet save for the noise of the dying traffic along Scotts Road and Orchard Road, and the occasional footfall of passers-by. Just another long, lonely night, he thought to himself.

Then it came. Loud and sharp and sudden. Manuel hurried to the source of the explosion, which was the Gents. He reached the toilet and saw smoke billowing out from it. As he got to the entrance, waves of intense heat emanating from within drove him back. There was no way he could put the fire out alone. Manuel rushed to the phone and called the police. Firemen arrived and prevented the fire from spreading to other areas of the building. The heat had damaged part of the ceiling and the cistern, and completely distorted the plastic seat of the bowl. However, what caught everyone's attention were the words scrawled on the wall:

RUNME SHAW   廿万元

INTENTION PARTY . . .

28th March 1976. Rangasamy, manager of Diamond Cinema, was taking stock of tickets for the 3.30 matinee when he was alerted of a fire at the store next door. Within minutes, the flames consumed a great part of the store and Rangasamy decided to cancel the show for fear of the safety of the patrons .

31st March 1976. Capitol was screening a movie on courageous heroes of China who fell like ten pins because they tried using martial arts to fight guns. Omar Kidam collected tickets to the Dress Circle seats. He had been on duty since three in the afternoon and he was collecting tickets for the last show of the day, which was at 9.30 p.m. Right after the movie began, Omar thought he'd have a little rest inside the auditorium, for he couldn't go off till midnight. So he went in and sat down.

Half an hour later, a sudden brightness burst up in the dark. Fear stabbed at his heart. A fire! he told himself. Before he could react, people inside the auditorium were already starting to stand up and stare at what was burning.

Then Omar saw him. He was already on his way out, his face concealed in the shadows. Omar sprang to his feet and sprinted after the man as fast as he could. His heart thumped excitedly. But as he got out of the auditorium, he fell. When Omar recovered, the man was gone. Meanwhile, a fireman on duty got an extinguisher and quickly doused the flames . . .

On those three occasions, the fires were contained before they could do serious damage. The arsonists ignited kerosene in either tin cans or bottles. Apparently, though, they weren't good at what they were doing, because they struck at insignificant places. But they were learning. And on 11th April 1976, at Queens Cinema, they graduated.

Mohamed Yasi, the ticket attendant, was collecting tickets for the last show of the day when a Chinese man, who had earlier entered the auditorium, came out and approached him.

'Ay, theatre very cold,' the man said. 'Air-conditioner too strong. Can you turn it down a bit?'

This wasn't the first occasion when a patron complained, and being only 20 yards away from the engine room, Yasin promptly went over to it and switched off the 30 HP plant. Hurrying back to collect tickets, he forgot to secure the padlock – no other attendant was around. While he was collecting tickets, his back was facing the engine room. Five minutes later, Yasin remembered: HE HAD FORGOTTEN TO LOCK THE ROOM! A sense of foreboding loomed over him and as he turned towards it he sighted a tall, good-looking youth flinging a lighted rag into the engine room. God! the bastard was going to destroy the engine plants! Yasin went after him. The chase lasted for a moment. The man got away.

This time, it cost the Shaw Organisation thirty thousand dollars.

Around noon the next day, manager of Queens Cinema, Chye Loo Chin heard the telephone in his office ringing. He picked up the receiver.

'Hello?'

'You the cinema manager?' The voice belonged to a man. He spoke in Hokkien.

'Yes. Who's that calling?' Chye asked.

'We are the *Daredevils*.'

A general view of the seats affected at Queens Cinema.

Chye was taken aback. *Daredevils*? Were they the ones responsible for the fire?

'The fire yesterday was caused by us.' The voice hardly gave Chye a chance to speak. 'Listen carefully, we are not afraid to burn another cinema if your boss does not agree to our terms. We will get the money from him even if we have to die for it.'

'What terms?' Chye asked.

'Don't ask. Your boss knows about it. You better send our message to your boss. We will call again tonight.'

Before Chye could enquire further, he heard the

click of the phone at the other end followed by the humming tone.

At 8.20 p.m. the *Daredevils* called again. This time, Yasin was in the office as well.

'What answer your boss given?' The voice asked.

'Just what do you think you are doing?' Chye replied, trying to divert the conversation. At the same time, he quickly signalled Yasin to contact the police and to get the call traced. 'You start fires and you think people will give you money to stop but have you ever thought you could hurt a lot of innocent people?'

The caller spouted a string of expletives before saying, 'You better not lecture me, understand? You think we like it?' The voice continued, 'We have to do it, understand? If we don't do it we might as well commit suicide. Anyway you better not talk too much. I'm giving you 24 hours to consider.'

The line went dead.

When Yasin returned some two minutes later, he said the police were unable to trace the call. There were no more calls for the next two days.

On 15th April at 11.30 a.m., Christine Tay, Runme Shaw's private secretary, heard the phone ring. She lifted the receiver.

'Mr Vee Meng Shaw in?' the voice said in fluent English.

'May I know who's speaking?' Christine asked, finding the voice unfamiliar.

'This is your friendly firebug, Intention Party. The fires at the cinemas, remember? I shall be brief. All we ask is two hundred thousand, or do you need further evidence of our – pyromania?'

Christine had earlier been briefed by Shaw on what to say should the arsonists call and now she told him, 'You're wasting your time!'

'I wouldn't interfere in my boss's affairs if I were you,' the man said. 'Please, for your own sake, keep out.'

The man hung up.

At 3.13 p.m. the same voice called again on a different line.

'Good afternoon, I wish to speak with Runme Shaw,' he said.

'Mr Shaw is not available now,' she replied.

'You had better have him speak with me. Tell him I'm one of the *Daredevils*,' he said. 'Your boss is indeed very stubborn. Tell him if our demands are not met we would raise the price to – half a million?'

'Do whatever you like,' Christine was frightened but she tried sounding angry. 'We aren't going to pay you.'

Inspector Oh Chye Bee was assigned to investigate the matter. Oh decided that the only way to nab the guys was to set a trap for them using money as bait. One week after the call to Chye, he approached Mr P. C. Seah, cinema supervisor for Shaw's Organisation.

'Anything I can do for you just ask,' Seah offered.

'Yes, I'd appreciate it if you could inform all your cinema managers to contact me should the extortionists call again.'

'I'd be glad to.'

Oh didn't have to wait long. On Tuesday, 20th

April, Oh was informed by Chye, manager of Queens that the extortionists had called, again threatening to burn down all the Shaw cinemas unless their demands were met. They said they would call on that day. Oh waited at the cinema office. Sure enough, the call came through. Chye answered the phone.

'Hold on,' Chye told the man. 'Runme Shaw's representative is here.'

Chye passed the receiver to Inspector Oh.

'This is Mr Oh speaking. I'm representing Runme Shaw.'

'Mr Oh, you've seen what we're capable of. All we ask is two hundred thousand dollars. The well-being of your cinemas depends on your cooperation.'

'Let's talk it over,' Oh said. 'Two hundred thousand is too much. How do I know you will not stop burning down the cinemas after you get the money?'

'We don't want to talk. I'll call again,' he said and hung up abruptly.

Oh received three more calls that day which repeated the same threat. It was as if there was more than one party involved. Their hanging up suddenly could mean that they weren't sure if it was the right time to ask for payment. However, Oh failed to prolong the conversation long enough for the call to be traced.

The break came the next day. The call came in at eleven-fifteen in the morning.

'My boss has agreed to your demand. Two hundred thousand. No more.'

'Good,' the voice said. Oh could almost see the

man smiling. 'I knew he'd come to his senses soon enough.'

'How and where do you want to collect the money?'

'Here are the instructions. Listen well. You are to withdraw the money from the bank this Saturday. It must be cash, in fifties and hundreds, as stated in our letter. We want old notes, unmarked, no running numbers, follow?'

'Yes.' Oh ground his teeth.

'After you've got the cash, you are to return to the cinema and await further instructions. One more thing. You will not withdraw the cash before hearing from us.'

Oh did some quick thinking. If they wanted him to go to Queens with the money, there might be a chance they'd collect the money there. That part about awaiting further instructions was, according to criminal parlance, to throw him off the track. Oh decided to play his hunch.

9.00 a.m. Saturday, 24th April, 1976. AOC Henry Thomas and a party of detectives stationed themselves inside the cinema. 9.40 a.m. The phone rang. Oh was to leave for the bank now. He was allowed to take only one person with him. Detectives followed.

10.15 a.m. Oh entered the bank at Shaw Towers. Wads of paper cut into sizes of fifties and hundreds were given to him in a plastic bag. Everything had to look real. Every action had to be played out as if money was genuine. The gang would in all probability be watching his movements. Detectives escorted Oh on the way back to Queens.

'Very good,' the voice on the phone said. 'I see you're cooperating well. Unfortunately, I see you are not alone. You will be where you are now tomorrow at about noon.'

The next day was Sunday. At twelve, the telephone rang and the voice Oh grew to hate spoke.

'You are to proceed to Swan Coffee House at Selegie Road and wait for instructions. Be there in twenty minutes.'

Oh cursed angrily at the way they were making a monkey out of him. They were playing a calculated game. They were careful criminals. He took the money and drove towards Swan Coffee House. Henry Thomas and his squad covered the place.

12.40 p.m. The phone rang.

'Excellent! Look under the phone. You will see a note and a map. Follow the instructions. After you've done so, come back here and wait for another call. While you do so, you may have a cup of coffee, unless of course duty does not permit you to drink during working hours.'

The note told Oh he had three minutes to place the money in the Ministry of Environment dustbin on the traffic island at the junction of Penang Road and Dhoby Ghaut.

Oh breathed with relief. So finally they were getting somewhere. He was getting tired of playing courier to those sons of bitches. But the case was far from over. The next thing now was to apprehend them.

The traffic island wasn't difficult to find. It was opposite Cathay cinema and about fifty metres from the coffee house. Thousands of people pass by it every day. Two Angsanas shaded the area and shrubbery sprouted here and there. Oh hurried to the spot and found, as indicated in the map, the dustbin. The bin was the Ministry of Environment type, slightly larger than an ordinary one, but rectangular instead of round. A semi-cylindrical top covered it so rubbish could be thrown into it only from the sides.

Oh walked over to the bin and dumped the bag inside. Then he made his way back to Swan Coffee House via Penang Road and Plaza Singapura, which was part of the instructions. All this time, Henry

Traffic island along Stamford Road, towards the direction of Penang Road/Orchard Road/Dhoby Ghaut.

Thomas and men kept watch. They were probably not the only ones watching.

'I'd like to thank you, Mr Oh, for being so cooperative. Tell your boss he will not regret this. You're free to go now.'

As soon as Oh hung up he and Inspector Roger Yeo drove towards Nicoll Highway. They made a change of clothes and headed for Penang Road. He parked the car and positioned himself near Supreme House.

The ambush was set. Henry Thomas's squad had been lying in wait since Oh deposited the bag in the bin. Roads leading to the traffic island were carefully watched. The extortionists would have to depend a lot on speed if they wanted to get away. But the roads were well covered, and the police well armed. And the thought of the way they had him running around made Oh more determined to get them. Oh could feel his heart beating fast. The suspense was killing him and he took deep breaths to calm himself. He only hoped that none of his men would be spotted and identified. If any of them were then the birds would fly and the scenario would have to be completely restaged.

They waited.

Eyes were trained on the traffic island.

It could be any time now.

After thirty minutes, nobody came.

Oh looked at the time restlessly. Why the hell were they taking so long? Maybe they were playing a waiting game. But Oh was willing to wait. Working in the force had taught him that patience and hard work would be rewarded. Criminals in the real world were not caught by ingenious, smart-aleck deductions and theorizing. Hard work was the main factor.

2.10 p.m. The police had been waiting nearly one and a half hours. No one turned up. Oh began to feel that this was just another of the crooks' ruses, meant to make them run round in circles. Or worse still, they had been spotted. Or worse still . . .

2.15 p.m. Doubts that they would come for the money grew stronger and stronger.

At 2.25 p.m., Oh started walking over to the bin. An unpleasant premonition kept nibbling at his mind. If the gang chose to appear now and saw him, that would be the end. Another time, another place.

He reached the traffic island. He walked towards the dustbin. His hand reached into the bin.

It was empty.

Oh looked with dread into the dustbin. The plastic bag containing the money wasn't there any more. There was a hole at the bottom of the bin. The bin itself was placed on top of an uncovered manhole. The manhole was connected to the monsoon drain.

On examination, a hole had earlier been made at the bottom of the bin. In its place was a false bottom with a latch which opened from the outside. The manhole itself was actually too large and would be noticed so a wooden frame was fitted into it, covering half of it. Earth was shoved on top of it till it blended neatly with the ground. The bin was then positioned directly above what remained of the hole.

The criminals were clever. And they were never caught.

The dustbin had a false bottom, through which the money was spirited away.

Manhole at close quarters. When the earth was brushed away, a wooden frame was revealed. This was used to reduce the size of the manhole so that it could be completely concealed by the dustbin.

CORPUS DELICTI

On a day in May, a woman was alone in her house when her sister-in-law came to see her. The sister-in-law was fifty-three years old, nearly ten years older than the woman herself. At the house, the visitor, dressed in a floral blouse and brown slacks, left her sandals outside, entered, and went into the dining room. The woman went in after her.

'You have the money?' the sister-in-law asked. The woman had borrowed $2,000 from her sister-in-law, who had in turn borrowed it from another woman; and the money was supposed to be returned to the original lender that day.

'I don't have the money,' the debtor replied. 'I'll get it in a few days.'

'But I need the money right now,' the older woman said, raising her voice. 'I have to return it.'

The woman became angry and shouted back. A quarrel ensued, then a fight. The sister-in-law punched her in the right eye. She felt a sharp pain and a dizziness. She fell on her knees, using her hands to cushion the fall. As she did so, she sprained her right thumb and bruised her knees; her head hit something hard. She became confused; she stood up and suddenly pounced at her sister-in-law, her hands caught the sister-in-law's neck, then tightened their grip. Somehow she lost control of herself, she didn't release her grip, nor did she notice whether her sister-in-law struggled or not.

After a long time, she realised her sister-in-law was quite motionless. She dragged her by her legs into the bathroom at the back of the house. Then she went to the kitchen and took out a chopper.

Back in the bathroom, she severed the victim's head from the body by slicing the flesh of the neck until she reached the vertebra, then chopping hard several times to cut through the bone. She did the same thing to the arm and legs. When that was finished, she chopped the torso into two. After butchering the body, she washed her hands and legs, went to a room next to the kitchen and got some plastic bags. When she came back to the bathroom, the floor of which was red with blood, she put the arms into the first bag, the head into the second, one half of the torso into the third, the other into the fourth, and the legs into the fifth. Bringing the first, second and fifth bags to another bathroom upstairs, she hid them between the tub and the wall. She went downstairs again, brought up the third bag containing half the torso, covered it with a gunny sack, and put that in an earthen jar, also in the upstairs bathroom. Just outside the downstairs bathroom, she inverted another earthen jar over the fourth plastic bag. That done, she washed the bathroom of the blood. The victim's clothes were then washed, too, before being put into another plastic bag. The dead woman's dentures and clothes buttons she wrapped in her (the dead woman's) handkerchief, put that in her (dead woman's) handbag which was in the dining hall, and the handbag in a cupboard upstairs. She searched for the victim's shoes, couldn't find them and presumed that they had been stolen, which wasn't unusual in her neighbourhood.

Everything was done by 2.30 p.m., three and a half hours since the victim stepped into the house.

At 5.40 p.m. on the ninth day of May, 1974, Sim Joo Keow's husband returned home. He noticed her bruised eye and sprained thumb.

'What happened to your eye and your thumb?' he asked.

'What?'

'Your eye? What happened to your eye?'

'I fell while washing the floor,' she said.

'Why don't you see a doctor?' he suggested.

'No,' she said. 'It's all right.'

Later that evening, her children returned home, saw what had happened to their mother, asked her the same questions. At her eldest daughter's insistence, Joo Keow went to Outram Road General Hospital to be examined by a doctor.

That same night, when Kwek Lee Eng failed to return home, her husband and children decided to make a police report at Paya Lebar Police Station. After making the report, they drove to three government hospitals to check if Lee Eng had been admitted for an accident injury. It was a vain attempt, and they came home around midnight to find Sim Joo Keow's husband waiting for them – he had earlier been informed of his sister's sudden and unexpected disappearance.

'Any news?' he asked.

'No, nothing so far,' Lee Eng's husband said wearily. 'We've made a police report and checked hospitals.'

'She might have been kidnapped,' Sim's husband suggested.

The men spoke till one in the morning, then Sim's husband went home.

The next day, two sons of Kwek Lee Eng, Sim's sister-in-law, came to her house. 'Our mother didn't come home last night,' one of them said. 'According to our grandmother, mother said she was coming here to settle some money matters or something. Grandmother said that around ten plus yesterday morning you called three times and asked for mother.'

'She didn't come here,' Sim told them.

Other relatives began arriving, too. All asked after the disappearance of Kwek Lee Eng.

'But she wasn't here,' Sim answered them again.

Then one of them asked, 'How did you bruise your eye?'

'I had a fall,' she said quietly.

By noon, the relatives left. She was alone again, and she waited.

Three o'clock. Time to act. Taking out the plastic bags containing the arms and the head, she put them into another larger plastic bag. Carrying them out in the streets, she hailed a taxi and told the driver to head for Geylang. As the taxi was reaching Sir

Arthur's Bridge, Kallang, she alighted. She walked to the middle of the bridge and threw the bags over the bridge. Then she took another taxi home.

There was no time to waste. She carried the bag with the legs, boarded the taxi and told the driver, 'Aljunied Road.'

Along Aljunied Road she had the driver stop the car. She paid him, got out, and walked to an area where some houses had been demolished. Going in, she continued walking till she came to an unoccupied hut. The plastic bag was flung into it.

Returning home in another taxi, she discovered that there was still no stench coming from the rest of the dismembered parts, but she didn't know where else to dispose of them. She couldn't do it now, because her husband and children would be home any minute.

The same night, the police phoned Sim Joo Keow's family and requested them to go down to Paya Lebar Police Station. Questioned by Inspector Tan Nguan Ker, Sim revealed:

[On 9 May 74 at about 9.30 a.m., my sister-in-law, Kwek Lee Eng phoned me to tell me that the couple who took a loan from her were coming down to pay her the money. She also told me to wait for her at the bus stop along Jalan Besar at 11.00 a.m.

At about 10.00 a.m., when my sister-in-law did not call my house, I rang her up at her house. Her mother-in-law answered the telephone and told me that Lee Eng was on her way. At about 11.00 a.m., I closed my house door and left for the bus stop along Jalan Besar. I waited for a few minutes before seeing my sister-in-law alighting from a bus service no. 83. Both of us then waited for the man in question.

A short while later, a car SW 2579E, came alongside. Lee Eng spoke to the occupants, a man and a woman, giving them directions to my house. Both of us then went to my house. The said car entered into Hindu Road leading to my house. I opened the main gate of the house and entered.

The man parked the car in the parking lot along Rowell Road in front of house No. 73. They then came into the house. My sister-in-law and I were in the hallway leading to the kitchen. Lee Eng asked if they'd brought the money. The man said they hadn't.

My sister-in-law began to scold the man, calling him an animal or something because he had promised to pay the money but did not keep the promise.

The man said again that he didn't have the money. My sister-in-law scolded the man again for not keeping his promise. The man was angry. The next instant the other woman grabbed hold of my sister-in-law. I was then standing immediately behind the man who turned round and punched me in the right eye. I fell to a kneeling position on the floor, using my left hand to cushion the fall. Hence the injuries on my left wrist (fingers and thumb) and both knees.

The man went straight to the kitchen and I ran out to the hall. I heard the knife being pulled out from the shelf. I don't know what took place after that except that I heard my sister-in-law shouting for help.

I walked out of the house and stood near the roadside near to Jalan Besar Road. I stood there at the same spot for more than an hour, not knowing what to do. It didn't occur to me to call the police or shout for help.

After more than an hour, I walked back to my house, about seventy feet away, I saw the couple walking away towards the field in front of my house. The main door of my house was locked and I had to use the key to open it. Entering, I saw blood stains in the room near the front hall, the stairs and the bathroom. The meat chopper was wet and put back in its place.

I took a piece of cloth and cleaned away all the blood stains. I did not tell my husband about the incident as I was frightened that he would know about the business I was doing. I lied to my husband that I sustained the injuries as a result of a fall . . .

I don't know whether the couple who came to my house on 9.5.74 did in fact owe my sister-in-law any money or not. I learned of the money business only when my sister-in-law asked the couple whether they brought the money or not. I have never seen the couple prior to that incident. I am unable to recognise any one of the couple. Descriptions of the couple:

Man: late forties, about five feet six, stout, normal complexion, normal hair style with receding hair-line, wears black spectacles.

Girl: late forties, five feet three, medium build, normal complexion, wearing brown colour dress.

The man was wearing a T-shirt and long trousers . . .]

#####

11th May, 1139 hrs. Inspector Wee Tzu Kiang of Beach Road Police Station received a call from the Duty Officer of 'Radio Division'. 'A pair of human legs were found at the common toilet at Lorong Sungkai, off Aljunied Road,' the DO told him. 'Please check it out.'

After informing his OC of the case, Wee set off for Lorong Sungkai with Inspector Go Heng. At the scene, he met PC 3317. PC 3317 had been informed by a group of people living in the area that a pair of human legs had been found. The policemen went into the hut nearby. At a corner, sticking out from the plastic bag, was a pair of feet.

State pathologist Dr Chao Tzee Cheng was called in at 1316 hrs. Examining the body, he said that the legs were a woman's, Chinese, and had been cut off after she had been killed less than 24 hours ago. The police conducted a search for other missing parts using a police dog. Nothing was found.

Meanwhile Inspector Tan Nguan Ker, who had interviewed Sim, had not managed to elicit any more information about the murder and released her from the station. Sim then called her husband at his uncle's house.

'I want you to go home,' he told her, not wanting any more trouble. 'I'll be back soon.'

Later, when he returned home, he found her sleeping on the sofa. Without disturbing her, he went to the back of the house to get himself a drink. After finishing the drink, he thought he'd feed his birds, so he walked towards the earthen jar to get some bird seeds.

What he saw shocked him: Blood stains, and

flies buzzing all over. He quickly ran back to the house and phoned the police.

Inspector Tan Peng Huat arrived with a team of officers. He was told that Inspector Tan Nguan Ker had interviewed Sim the night before, and he questioned her again.

'I didn't kill her,' Sim said. 'A man and a woman came to the house supposedly to pay my sister-in-law money. When they told her they hadn't the money, she began to abuse them. The man then killed her and I was forced to conceal the body. But I've thrown the body away.'

'Who are they?' Tan asked. 'What are their names?'

'I don't know,' was the reply.

Inspector Tan was then led to the overturned earthen jar. The stench of a decomposing body came from it. Overturning the jar, he found a plastic bag. Inside that was half a torso.

Fifteen minutes later, he was informed of another stench emanating from the bathroom upstairs. Apparently, Sim had not told him everything. He went back to her.

'There's a stench coming from the bathroom upstairs,' he asked. 'Can you explain that?'

'The other half of the body is there,' she said. 'But I didn't kill her.'

'What do you know about this?' he asked.

'I wasn't involved in the killing,' she said, maintaining her stand. 'I told you, the man and the woman were responsible for killing her.'

Twenty minutes after the body was found, Dr Chao arrived to examine the human parts. The

General view of the shed, showing Aljunied Road in the background. The road where the cars are parked is Lorong Sungkai.

Inverted earthen jar in the bathroom on the upper floor. Photograph was taken after the marble table was removed.

turning point in the case occurred at 4.15 p.m. Inspector Tan was by the air well where half the body had been found when Detective Lionel came up to him.

'The suspect wants to speak with you,' Lionel said.

* * * * * * * * * * * * * * * * * * *

A police statement is given voluntarily. There is a rule that officers of the law should not allow the accused to confess to a crime until he or she has been officially charged with the crime, made to understand that he is being charged, cautioned, and has signed the caution sheet.

Inspector Tan went into the living room and approached Sim.

'I wish to tell you everything about the killing,' she said. By that time, perhaps she realised she couldn't hide the truth any longer. But no sooner had she begun to confess to the murder than Tan stopped her.

He read to her in Teochew the charge of murder under Section 302, Cap. 103, and after she said that she knew what it meant, both of them signed the charge sheet. Next, he repeated the same procedure, this time reading the caution. When they had signed that, he recorded her statement.

The recording ended at 4.55 p.m. Tan read Sim's statement and she confirmed it was correct. Sim then led Tan upstairs to the earthen jar that lay beneath a marble table. In it was the other part of the body.

Bringing him to the room in front, she said that the clothes of the dead woman were in the cupboard. The chopper was also shown to the police.

Subsequently, Sim brought Inspector Tan and his team to Kallang and indicated the spot on the bridge where she had hurled the bag containing the head and arms.

Then she brought them to Aljunied Road. Leading Tan to the hut, she showed him where she had flung the bag with the legs.

Back at Kallang, divers searched the river, but at first it couldn't be found. Then someone smelled that same decomposing odour as that in the house, and searching, saw the plastic bag – hanging on a tree: when Sim threw it over Sir Arthur's Bridge, it somehow got caught on a branch.

The last parts of the body were finally found.

There is a discrepancy in the account given by Sim Joo Keow and police findings as to who owed who money. Sim had told the investigator that it was Kwek Lee Eng who owed her money. That fateful day, when Kwek went to her house, she had asked Kwek for the money. Kwek, in a loud voice, said she didn't have the money, and suddenly punched Sim. That's how the fight began. But police investigations revealed that it was Sim who had borrowed $2,000 from Kwek, who had in turn borrowed it from one Lim Chia Yim. Chia Yim said that when she asked Kwek for the return of her money, the latter told her that she (Kwek) had lent the money to Sim. Kwek had earlier asked Sim for the money, but Sim said that the cheque had to be cashed into an account before the money could be withdrawn – police found a cheque of $3,000 in Sim's drawer. Also, since 1973, Sim had been pawning her jewellery without ever redeeming them.

Dr Chao Tzee Cheng performed an autopsy on the body, and concluded that the cause of death was by strangulation.

Sim Joo Keow pleaded guilty to manslaughter and was sentenced to 10 years' imprisonment.

THE MOUNT VERNON HORROR

On the night of 21st April 1978, three friends, Ong Chin Hock, Yeo Ching Boon and Ong Hwee Kuan, all twenty years old, came out of the billiard room at Kallang Amusement Centre and walked to the Geylang Bahru children's playground. They sat at the playground and chatted quite aimlessly, wandering from one topic to another and quite expectedly, the conversation led to how hard life was: Ching Boon and Hwee Kuan were unemployed and Chin Hock was serving his national service. They were broke and they were unhappy and they wanted money.

'Life would be much easier if only we have money,' one of them said. 'With money, we can do nearly anything.'

'Talking about it sounds so good,' another one added, 'what about some action? How are we going to get money?'

After a moment, Kuan, who had a rough face and a flat nose remarked loudly, 'I know how! We rob!' The others looked at him. 'We could get together and rob somebody,' he said.

Then Yeo said, 'Yes, why not? We need money, right?' His neat haircut and innocent face lent an air of civility to his appearance.

'How do we do it?' Hock asked. He had drooping eyes and sported a thin, fine moustache.

'I know, first we need a gun. This is important: to commit robbery these days you need a gun,' Kuan answered, as if he had been contemplating the idea long before.

'Yes, we'll need a gun,' Hock said. 'Ay! I think I know how to get a gun! And easily too!' Yeo said. 'There's a police sentry on duty at Mount Vernon PRU Base. I've performed duty there before during my NS. We could steal the gun from him. The best time to steal the gun would be in the middle of the night, that is when the men tend to be lax.'

'But there is a problem,' Yeo continued. 'How are we going to take the gun from him without attracting attention?'

Hock and Kuan had been listening and now they gave a few suggestions on how they could divest the policeman of his revolver. One by one, they examined the various possibilities, slowly, carefully. None was feasible. By eleven o'clock, they came up with nothing substantial and decided to go home. Yeo said, 'Better think of how we can do it. We need money, remember.'

The three men had been childhood friends, having attended Tu Li Primary School together. Ong Chin Hock, known to his parents and friends as Ah Hock, was single and lived at New Upper Changi Road. His father was a construction labourer, his mother a housewife. Sadly, Chin Hock didn't know her name. In school, he was not interested in his work and played truant. When he reached Primary 3, he left school and began to work as an odd job labourer, then as a hawker assistant and a construction worker, until he enlisted in the army.

Yeo Ching Boon, known as Ah Pui or Freddy by his friends, lived with his parents. He was the eldest of a family of three boys and a girl. In Secondary 3, Tu Li Secondary School, he was expelled for fighting. He found a job as a Stock Handler at Ma Li Textile Company. Three months later, he was sacked from Ma Li – again for fighting. He then worked as a fitter in Jurong and, after the job was done, as a wireman for which he was paid about $200/- a month. Then came his national service, which he served as a policeman at PRU Base at Mount Vernon Road.

Chin Hock and Ching Boon weren't associated with any secret societies. Hwee Kuan was. Friends and parents called him Ah Kuan. His father was the co-owner of a coffee stall and his mother a washer-woman. He had never passed any of his examinations from Primary 1 till Primary 4, and only managed to reach the next standard through automatic promo-. tions. In 1972, after failing his Entrance Examination the second time, he stopped schooling. Since then, he had worked as a painter and an odd job labourer at various worksites, earning very little pay; and associ-ated with members of the 'Sio Kun Tong' of the '18' group which operated at Angullia Road. He and other gang members had committed a series of pick-pocketing.

In February 1973, he (Kuan) was placed under police supervision for a year for being associated with the secret society. In June 1973, he was arrested, charged and sentenced to two years' imprisonment for consorting with another Police Supervisee. When released, he was again placed under supervision for another year. Some time in 1976, he, Chin Hock and another friend robbed a Malay man of his wrist watch and $18/- cash. They sold the wrist watch for $30/- and each of them pocketed $16/-. On top of this, he also smoked heroin. And in April 1977, he was sent to the Drug Rehabilitation Centre at Telok Pakau for 6 months' detention.

In the afternoon the next day, the three met again in the billard room at Kallang Amusement Park, then proceeded to the hawker centre below the billiard room for lunch. After lunch, they took a taxi to Lorong Koo Chye to visit a couple of friends, but found none of their friends there. It was past four o'clock and they sauntered to Tu Li Primary School to watch a football game.

At the Tu Li school field, Yeo brought up the robbery idea and asked them if they would like to go to a quiet corner to discuss the matter.

'Are you all still willing to join me in robbing the policeman's gun?'

They were.

'Before we can get the gun, we need weapons to threaten the police. I suggest – icepicks,' Yeo said.

'I think we should use knives too,' Kuan said.

'But we need money to buy the knives,' Yeo added. 'I have no money for that.'

Hock said, 'Pawn my watch and use the money.'

Yeo nodded and continued, 'I've already thought of the plan. This is what we do: I'll wear my police uniform; Hock, you wear your army one; Kuan, you be in civilian; like that it is easier to approach the sentry.'

'No, we cannot do it so openly,' Hock said after a moment's consideration. 'There is a camp guard there. He might get attracted by the uniforms and try to give us some trouble. We cannot approach the sentry so directly.'

'What then?' Yeo asked, dejectedly.

They arrived at another dead end. They discussed how they could rob the sentry of his gun without being spotted, but came up with nothing.

'I think it's okay,' Yeo said finally. 'We might not be spotted after all. Let's take the risk. We need a lot of money for our lives to be easy, right? We shall carry out the plan at 2.00 a.m. on the night after tomorrow.'

Hock then removed his Titoni watch from his wrist and handed it to Yeo.

The sky was getting dark and they had dinner at a nearby coffee shop before enjoying themselves at a Trade Fair at Paya Lebar Road.

The next day was Monday. Yeo and Kuan pawned Hock's Titoni at a shop in Serangoon for $15/-. At 5.30 p.m. Hock left camp and with Kuan, met Yeo at the Kallang billiard room. Yeo was having a game with a couple of friends and the two friends watched the entire game so it wasn't till nine o'clock that they went to a SILO emporium and Yeo bought two kitchen knives.

'It's still early,' Yeo said. 'Dangerous carrying

these weapons around – some nosy policeman might spot us and check on us. I'd better keep the knives at home first.'

Hock and Kuan waited while Yeo took the knives home. In the flat, Yeo cut a yellow nylon rope into four pieces. He put the ropes, knives, an icepick and a pair of gloves in his younger brother's travelling bag. Ten minutes later, he joined his friends. There were still four hours to kill before they could go ahead with the plan.

'We need some money for transport,' Yeo said.

'I could borrow some from my friends,' Hock said; and he and Kuan left by bus for Lorong Koo Chye to carry out the task. They met again at 11.45 p.m. at Kallang Bahru. Hock had not obtained any money but Yeo managed to borrow ten dollars from a friend. And they spent part of it on Char Kuay Teow and coffee.

After the meal, Yeo said, 'Are you ready? Here is the plan: we have to get a taxi. We tie the driver up and Hock will drive to the main gate of the base. Kuan, you will play drunk at the rear seat and I'll approach the sentry for help. I'll lure him to the taxi. Then we abduct him, bring him to a lonely spot and take his revolver away.'

'You're not going to let the driver and the policeman go, are you?' Kuan said. 'I mean it's not safe. I have a police record. The policeman or the driver may recognise me and identify me later.'

'All right,' Yeo said. 'Better if we play safe. They must die.'

Kuan felt better at the suggestion.

Hock listened and kept quiet.

At one-thirty in the morning, they left the coffee shop. Yeo went back home, changed to a red T-shirt and dark blue pants – they had abandoned the idea of the uniforms – and came back with the travelling bag. On the way, he had taken the icepick out and tucked it into the front of his pants. Hock was wearing white long sleeves and dark blue pants, and Kuan wore beige long sleeves and blue jeans.

'Ready?' Yeo asked.

'Ready.'

'Ready.'

The three friends walked near Block 66 at Kallang Bahru and waited for a cab to come by . . .

Chew Theng Hin got into his taxi, started it, turned on the headlights, and began driving off. It was one-forty in the morning, the time at which he normally left his home at Selegie House. He plied in the early hours of the morning; in the day, he hired the taxi, his own, out to two friends. Chew was sixty years old with a crew cut and stubbles growing on his chin and above his upper lip. Most men his age would have retired, but he still kept going.

This night, he decided to go in the direction of Kallang Bahru. He drove slowly, keeping a look-out for passengers. Shortly, as he was passing Block 66, he spotted three men who signalled him to stop. He pulled over. The front door opened and one of them dropped next to him. The other two came in the back and sat quietly. Then the one in front, apparently the leader, said, 'Police Reserve Unit, Mount Vernon Road.'

Chew went by way of Bendemeer Road, Whampoa East, Serangoon Road, and Upper Aljunied

Road. As he approached the PRU Base, the man in front directed him to keep left. The area along which he was driving was dark, quiet. When the taxi reached the rear gate, the leader said, 'Stop here.' Chew brought the vehicle to a standstill.

The second man behind caught him by the neck and placed the blade of the knife at his neck. The leader jammed a piece of cloth into his mouth, pointed an icepick at him and said, 'Don't make any noise.' He brought out some nylon ropes from his rear pocket and tied Chew's hands. Chew's body began to shudder in terror. The third man got down the car and opened Chew's door.

'Get down!' the leader ordered.

By some instinct, Chew knew these men weren't just going to let him go, even if he had given them his full cooperation. If he made a dash for it, maybe he could still save himself. With a sudden spurt of physical exertion, he tried to break loose from them.

The first and third men caught him. The second man slid the knife into his stomach. Chew moaned at the sharp pain.

The leader pulled him by the shoulders and the second man by the legs. They got him out of the taxi and pushed him into a drain. The third man got into the driver's seat and reversed the vehicle. Chew crawled out of the drain. The leader and the second man saw him. The leader had his icepick with him. The second man a knife. They went up to Chew. The icepick and knife sank into Chew's neck. Chew tumbled back into the drain.

The two men returned to the car. Before it moved off, they noticed Chew clambering out once more. The leader and the second man came out and stabbed him again in the vital regions. This time, Chew never came out.

That second man, the one who participated in the cruel killing of an almost helpless sixty-year-old man, was Ong Hwee Kuan. The leader, the brains behind the entire operation, was Yeo Ching Boon.

The first part of the job was done. Hock manoeuvred the taxi slowly towards the PRU Base. In a minute, he stopped in front of the PRU I main gate at Mount Vernon . . .

Lee Kim Lai was eighteen years old, the second child in a family of three boys and two girls. He was attached to the Police Reserve Unit at Mount Vernon for his national service. On 25th April 1978, the troop K.I.C. Police Reserve Unit I was on Emergency duty. Each sentry was issued his .38 Webley & Scott revolver and ten rounds of ammunition. At 2.00 p.m., Kim Lai relieved his predecessor, Koh Kah Kway, who had been on duty since 1.00 a.m. Not long after he had taken over, Kim Lai saw a yellow and black taxi come up to the gate.

Kuan lay on the rear seat and played drunk. Yeo came up to Kim Lai and flashed his NS Police Warrant card. 'My friend and I are from this Reserve Unit,' Yeo said to Kim Lai. 'We had a few drinks earlier and he took more than he should have . . . he is lying at the back of the car now. Can you please help me carry him out?'

Lai looked at the card, then at the stranger. 'Are you residing at the PRU Base?' he asked.

'Yes,' Yeo lied, pointing at the taxi whose motor

was still running. He had the icepick tucked at his waist.

Kim Lai, who felt it was one's civic duty to help a fellow man, opened one side of the gate and followed Yeo. They came to the back door of the vehicle. Yeo acted fast. Opening the left rear door, he shoved Kim Lai in. The icepick was out the next instant.

'Don't resist and don't raise an alarm,' Yeo told Kim Lai. As he was returning to the front seat, Yeo saw two figures at the first and second floor of the Police Quarters and they appeared to be looking at him. He got in, slamming the door shut. Hock reversed the taxi and sped off towards Aljunied Road.

'Hurry!' Yeo yelled at Hock. 'I think somebody at the police station has seen us!'

Kuan was sitting with Kim Lai at the back. He held his knife out.

'Where's the other knife?' Yeo asked Kuan. Kuan pointed to the hump between the two front seats. Yeo picked it up.

The car swung left from Mount Vernon Road to Upper Aljunied Road.

'I have no money! I have no money!' Kim Lai kept saying, shaking his head fearfully.

Kuan pushed the knife into Kim Lai's neck.

The policeman wriggled, swinging his hands and legs wildly in mortal pain and in a desperate, pitiable attempt to fight back. Kuan drew the captive's revolver out and handed it to Yeo. When Kuan wanted to pull the knife out, he found the weapon was stuck. He yanked hard to dislodge the blade. Yeo then turned around and stabbed Kim Lai several times at the neck. Yeo wasn't careful when he swung the knife and he cut Kuan's index finger. Kim Lai slumped back on the seat. Blood founted around the seat and onto Kuan's shirt and pants.

'We must get rid of the weapons,' Yeo told Kuan. 'Give me your knife.' Kuan handed over his blade. Five minutes later, they were somewhere at Kallang Bahru when Yeo told Hock to stop the taxi.

There were five rounds in the revolver. Yeo rummaged the sentry's pockets and came up with five extra rounds.

'Pui,' Kuan said to Yeo, 'my clothes, they're red.'

'Go hide behind the bushes,' Yeo instructed him. 'I'll bring some clean clothes from home.'

Yeo and Hock left. Ten minutes later Yeo came back to the bushes where Kuan was still hiding. He passed a plastic bag containing a pair of dark blue shorts and a white T-shirt to Kuan. Kuan changed, dumping his blood-stained clothes into the bag.

About to leave, they stopped as a stranger suddenly came up to them . . .

Constable Siew Man Seng had been with the Force for eleven years. At the time of the events, he was attached to the Crime Branch of Beach Road Police Station. He had a wife and a daughter. Having been a resident of Geylang Bahru for the past four and a half years, he knew the area well.

On 25th April, at about 2.15 a.m., he left the police station after successfully arresting an offender in a forgery case an hour earlier. Man Seng drove homeward, satisfied with the day's work.

Reaching the junction of Kallang Bahru and Geylang Bahru, he saw the traffic light switch to red.

Man Seng's foot gently pushed the brake pedal and the car retarded slowly to a halt. Waiting for the green light to appear, he looked about and noticed a young man walk past the rear of his car and across the road towards a PUB Station. The man had a plastic bag with him.

The light turned green and Man Seng turned left into Geylang Bahru. As he did so he looked in his rear view mirror and found that the man had disappeared into the Geylang Bahru Road which led to a dead end. Years of experience as an investigator had somehow attuned his senses to suspect anything out of the ordinary, and Man Seng made a U-turn and headed in the direction where the man had disappeared. He drove slowly along the *cul-de-sac*, keeping a lookout for the man. As he passed the middle of the dead-end road, a yellow and black taxi came into view, the engine of which was still running. The end of the road was in sight and he turned the car around. Then he noticed bushes on the left.

Instincts told him to check the place.

He parked his car some distance off and threaded steadily to the bushes.

And saw the two men.

Yeo Ching Boon and Ong Hwee Kuan.

'What are you doing here,' Man Seng spoke loudly as he approached.

The men emerged from the bushes. One of them, Yeo, was the one he had seen earlier. Both had strong feelings that Man Seng was a man of the law.

Yeo unexpectedly dashed towards the SILO emporium. Kuan also started running towards Block 72 of Geylang Bahru.

Kuan ran in blind panic. He flew past the block of flats and came to an empty piece of land. The uneven ground undulated beneath his feet. He fell, got back on his feet, ran, fell again. Crossing the middle of the piece of ground, Kuan looked back.

The constable was catching up.

Some bushes were nearby. Kuan knew if he kept running there was no way he could outrun his pursuer. He quickly hid behind a bush. From there, he eyed the policeman closely. He was panting heavily, his heart thumping fast and hard.

The pursuer came, closer, closer. Relief overcame him as he watched the detective go past him.

Then dogs started barking.

The detective stopped.

He saw a patch of white behind the bushes.

He came towards the bushes.

Kuan's stomach turned over.

Man Seng drew out his revolver and pointed it at the bush.

'All right, get out!' he ordered Kuan.

Kuan came out. Man Seng took out his handcuffs and, with difficulty because the captive struggled, handcuffed him.

'Where's the bag you were carrying?' he asked.

'I threw it away while I was running.'

'You better bring me to it.'

Kuan led Man Seng to somewhere nearby but the bag had seemingly disappeared.

'What is in the bag?' Man Seng asked.

'A comb,' Kuan replied. 'My friend and I planned to rob you but when we found out you were a detective we ran.'

'What's your friend's name?'

'Ah Seng.'

Man Seng saw bloodstains on Kuan's shirt even though he had just changed.

'Why is there blood on your shirt?' he asked.

Kuan's mind raced for a good excuse.

He showed the detective his index finger which had earlier been cut by Yeo in the process of stabbing the sentry. 'Before you spotted me, I was breaking bottles in the bushes to use them as weapons,' he said. 'I got careless and cut myself.'

Man Seng didn't believe him. He continued to search for the bag. When he couldn't find it he decided to bring Kuan in for questioning.

Before reaching his car, Kuan, still in handcuffs, suddenly said, 'Wait, I'm thirsty, I need to have a drink.'

'There's no water around,' Man Seng replied.

Kuan indicated a pool of muddy water inside a small drain. 'I must drink,' he said and before Man Seng could stop him, he lurched forward into the pool and wet the front of his shirt more than he drank.

Later, while in the car on the way to the police station, Kuan said again, 'Please, I need to drink water.' Man Seng brought him to a hawker centre but he saw that Kuan, instead of drinking the water, was wetting the front of his shirt again.

Then he realised: The captive was trying to wash the bloodstains away!

'Stop!!' Man Seng shouted.

At the Beach Road Police Station Siew Man Seng informed the Duty Officer, Inspector Poh Keng How of the entire episode. Before they could interrogate

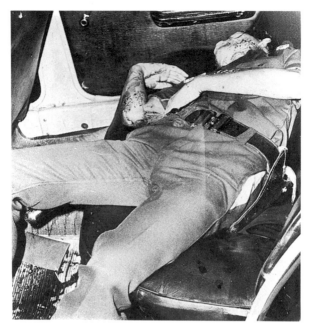

The deceased, Lee Kim Lai, in full police uniform, lying in the rear seat of taxi SH 3610 C. The gun holster at the left hip of the deceased was empty.

Kuan, Poh was told that a police sentry at Mount Vernon Road was found dead inside a taxi at Geylang Bahru.

He related all he knew to Inspector Cheok Koon Seng of the Special Investigation Section. Ong Hwee Kuan was interrogated but denied having had anything to do with the murder.

Then this happened:

7.20 a.m.: the body of Chew Theng Hin, the taxi driver, was discovered.

8.00 a.m.: the plastic bag that Man Seng had failed to locate was found. It contained a checked shirt, long-sleeved, and a pair of blue Hara jeans, both bloodstained. Ong Hwee Huat, Kuan's brother, confirmed that they belonged to his brother.

Contents of the travelling bag. There were two knives, an icepick, 3 pieces of nylon rope, a pair of black frame glasses, a piece of red cloth, a piece of paper, a pair of white gloves, and 2 pieces of a dollar note. The travelling bag was found about half a mile away from the abandoned taxi.

8.40 a.m.: Ong Hwee Kuan was told of the discovery of the taxi driver and his clothes and, when asked to allow his fingerprints to be taken to compare with those lifted from the taxi, admitted to being involved in the killings and gave the identity of Yeo Ching Boon.

12.50 p.m.: Yeo Ching Boon was arrested in his home. Under interrogation, he cracked and admitted his part in the murders. He then led the police to his house where he had hidden the Webley and the ten bullets. He then brought the police to the field of lallang where he had disposed of the travelling bag containing the knives, the icepick, a pair of spectacles, a pair of white gloves, a piece of red cloth, two dollars in cash, and three small rolls of orange nylon ropes.

8.30 p.m.: Ong Chin Hock, the driver of the stolen taxi, surrendered himself and confessed.

All three were tried and sentenced to death.

OF CRIME AND PASSION

Passion hurts, emotionally and physically. Sometimes, fatally. All it takes is a misdeed on the part of one and a misunderstanding on that of the other. Passion does the rest of the work: there is a confrontation, a heated argument perhaps, and before you know it, someone lies dead.

Crimes of passion are not confined to soap operas, they happen in real life; and the following is one. I apologise for revealing the denouement of this story at the beginning – it isn't a happy one, because the man finally killed the girl he loved and was sentenced to four years' imprisonment.

As a child, Hok used to go to the hawker centre at the junction of Tiong Bahru and Jalan Membina. His liking for the place remained with him to adulthood.

At this haunt, he met Sai Tok, but hardly associated with him, and only renewed his acquaintance with him in 1981. One day, on invitation, he visited Sai Tok's home at Jalan Membina, where they, with some other friends, had a game of mahjong. There, he came to know June, a nineteen-year-old girl who frequented Sai Tok's flat. She, too, lived near the hawker centre, and was usually in the company of Sai Tok, Sum Mau and Ah Lim.

Hok was then working as a service boy at People's Park, and during his spare time, started going to the flat often. One day in 1982 found him and June alone in the flat. They spoke; and when the initial shyness had worn off and they had grown more accustomed to each other, he asked, 'Would you like to go out with me?'

'Okay,' she said.

'But there's one thing I'd like you to know,' he said. 'If you're going steady with someone, I wouldn't want to come between you.'

'No,' she replied. 'I haven't taken anyone seriously, although I do go out with boys.'

'All right,' he said.

In time, they dated once a week, secretly, because Hok didn't want the people who frequented Sai Tok's flat to know. Four months later, he brought her to a brothel in Geylang where they spent the night.

He discovered to his dismay that she had had someone else before. She told him about her former boyfriend called Francis, who was then either doing time or in some rehabilitation centre because he had a drug problem; and that she, too, had taken drugs with Francis on occasions. She became angry with Francis because he had pushed her head against a wall and since then had not been on intimate terms with him.

Although shaken·by that knowledge, Hok realised that he was in love with her; it took him a long time, but he eventually got over it.

When he saw her again, he said, 'June, I like you a lot, and I'm willing to forget your past and be your steady if you could change your character, if you could refrain from . . .'

'I'll try my best not to fool around with other boys,' she said.

The courtship continued rather smoothly, without any violent quarrels.

Late one night in 1983, almost a year later, sitting at the hawker centre, he saw her walking home. He wanted to know where she had been and the company she was keeping, so he phoned her.

'Where did you go?' he asked.

'I went out with friends,' she answered, apparently evading the question.

'Those friends,' he asked. 'Are they boys or girls?'

The question annoyed her and she said, 'I went out with some friends. Please don't ask so many questions.'

The same thing happened again later, but he thought it better to forget it.

A year passed.

1st February 1984 was Lunar New Year's Eve, a day when nearly all Chinese families held their reunion dinners. At 5.00 p.m., Hok once again went down to the hawker centre after his morning shift to see if June was there, and if not, he'd still hang around anyway. There was some gambling on. He joined in and lost. At seven, he stopped playing and had a few drinks with his friends. But June still wasn't around.

By eleven that night, at a friend's suggestion, he joined a barbecue celebration at Kim Tian Hawker Centre and stayed there till nine the next morning because the rain prevented him from going home. When the rain cleared, he returned home and slept. Around noon, his mother woke him up. 'There's a girl who wants to speak to you on the phone,' she told him.

The girl turned out to be June.

'Hok,' she said. 'I can't see you today. I have to visit my grandmother.'

Again, Hok spent his day at Jalan Membina's hawker centre. At eleven the next morning, the second day of the Lunar New Year, they spoke on the phone.

'You came back late?' he asked.

'I came back at two this morning,' she told him. 'At my grandmother's house, I won some money gambling. Hok, have you any money?'

'No, I don't,' Hok said uneasily, remembering his loss the day before.

'I'll give you some,' she said. 'I'll give you $200/-.'

'Thanks,' he said. 'But I'll repay you when I get my pay.'

'I'm going down to the hawker centre this evening, at about six,' she said. 'Could you meet me?'

'All right.'

Hok was down by three that afternoon. But at six, she had not turned up. He waited, and it wasn't till past seven-thirty that she arrived. He was leaning against a staircase railing when he saw her walking with Ah Lim, a mutual friend; they were coming in his direction so he stood where he was; but she stopped suddenly at the area where some gambling called 'See Goh Luk' (meaning four five six) was going on. He realised that she might not have seen him but decided to wait. After fifteen minutes he became impatient, and, walking over to June, tapped her on the shoulder. She turned around, saw him, told him to wait a little while. He walked to another table and sat down. He didn't like the idea of her handing the $200 to him in public, and when she came five minutes later, he asked her to go with him behind the public toilets to hand it to him. Unseen behind the walls, she passed four fifty-dollar bills to him. After that, she returned to the gambling table while he made for a coffee stall.

A short time later, still sitting at the table of the coffee stall, he saw June walking with two of his friends, Ah Lim and Sum Mau; they were heading towards Kim Tian Hawker Centre and Hok assumed that June had wanted to go there for her favourite Fried Hokkien Mee. The sight of his girl in the company of his friends pained him. What's the matter with her, he thought. Why didn't she ask me to come along?

He sat thinking for some time, then stood up and walked to Kim Tian Hawker Centre to return her the $200. Somehow, he just didn't feel like holding money that came from her. When he got there he found her sitting with Ah Lim, in front of the Hokkien Mee stall. They had just finished their meal and she was smoking a cigarette. He came to her and quietly placed the money on her lap.

'Hok,' Lim said on seeing him. 'Come, join us.'

'No, thanks,' Hok said, and walked away quickly to the bus stop to wait for his bus, thinking of June all the time. When he reached the bus stop he thought of asking her to visit him, for it was the New Year. He went back to the stall; she was still there.

'June, could I speak to you alone,' he said to her.

They went near a public toilet behind the hawker centre.

'Did you get the $200 intact?' he asked.

'Yes, there's $200 altogether,' she answered. 'But why are you giving the money back to me?'

That moment, he didn't want her to know he had done it because he was hurt, and he said, 'A friend just returned me some money. Erh, June, are you going to my place tomorrow?'

'No, I don't think I want to.'

'Are you going out with Lim tonight?' he asked, noticing she was dressed up to go out and remembering that she once told him Lim was very fond of her.

'No, I'm not going out with Lim,' she said. 'I'm going to a birthday party in Ang Mo Kio.'

It wasn't a good time to discuss things, so Hok went home while June returned to the table.

At seven the next evening, he phoned her from Jalan Membina Hawker Centre.

'June,' he asked, 'could you lend me fifty dollars.'

'Sure,' she said. 'Hok, did you pawn the gold

chain and ring I gave you?'

'No, they're with me,' he answered. 'Listen, I'll go up to your place to get the money, all right?'

'Okay.'

June's flat was close to the hawker centre and Hok walked there. At the foot of the block, he saw a man he thought was Francis, June's former boyfriend, but he proceeded to go up to her flat, and waited for her outside. A minute later, she rushed out, pressed the money to his hand, and ran back inside. Hok supposed she didn't want her mother to catch her handing him money, so he went home.

On Sunday, 5th February '84, Hok was down again at the Jalan Membina Hawker Centre. It was two in the afternoon and he lingered there till eight before calling June. He was informed she wasn't in, so he guessed she was at Sai Tok's flat. He arrived at the flat and saw June seated with some of his friends. Sum Mau was standing behind her, touching her hair. He went into the flat.

'June,' he called from the kitchen. 'Can I speak with you in private?'

She agreed, and they went to the ground floor staircase.

'June, I need some money to see a doctor. I have a backache.' Then he noticed a mark that resembled a love bite on the right of her neck, just below her chin. This gave him a nasty surprise, because she had always told him not to give her any love bites.

'June,' he asked, 'how come you have a love bite on your neck?'

Her mood changed suddenly and she said coldly, 'If you think it's a love bite, then it's a love bite. Mind your own business and stop questioning me.'

In the past days, their relationship had already been like heavy weights hanging on a frayed string, and the thought that she had allowed that person to give her that bite was like that last, fatal ounce dropped lightly onto the weights.

His temper flared. His left hand shot out and pushed her neck against the wall, pinning her. His right hand swung into her abdomen. Then he grabbed her neck with both hands and shook her, saying, 'Why don't you go back home! Go back home and think of how you've been treating me! I've been treating you well! I've even made it a point of forgetting your past! Now I'll ask you again, how did you get that love bite? Someone from Sai Tok's place?'

'No, no, it isn't,' she answered, feebly.

'Go back home and think,' he said, and walked off.

His backache wasn't the only reason why he didn't go to work the next day; he applied for urgent leave through a colleague. Then he phoned her, and was told by her brother that she had not returned that night. Neither did she call him.

He wasn't feeling too well the day after either, and went to the Government clinic at Jalan Bukit Merah to have the doctor examine him. The doctor gave him medical leave for one day. When he got home, he called her several times, again to be told that she wasn't in.

On 8th February, his back still troubling him, he saw the company doctor who gave him one day off.

He went to his grandmother's house and phoned June. Although he got through to her, all she said was, 'I'm not free.'

He returned home and tried once more. She answered the phone but told him she was busy preparing for the 'god festival'.

He took the next three days off. At noon on the 9th, he made another call to her. The girl who answered the phone said she wasn't June, but he recognized her voice.

'June,' he said. 'I know it's you. Please, don't avoid me.'

'What do you want?' she asked.

'I'm sorry, June,' he said.

'Don't apologise to me,' she said. 'I'm not accepting it.'

'I'm sorry,' he said again.

'I told you, I'm not accepting it.'

'I know you're still angry with me,' he said. 'Maybe you should cool down first before we talk. I tell you what, I'll call you back in exactly one month's time, on 9th March, and we can discuss the matter.'

'It's up to you whether you wish to call me or not,' she said dampeningly, and hung up.

He quietly put the receiver down; he took out a photograph of June and her twin sister which she had given him in happier days and wrote '9th March 84' at the back of it.

On 13th February, he reported for work. At lunch time, he went to pawn the gold chain and ring June had given him – he needed the money to settle a debt. They gave him $200 for it.

Remembering that it was St Valentine's Day the

next day, he walked over to a florist opposite the Subordinate Courts and bought a rose for June, and asked to have it sent to June's address.

After work that day, he had a bottle of Guinness Stout and chatted with friends. An hour later, as he was about to leave, Florence Tan, a friend, invited him to gamble at Sai Tok's flat. He agreed, and at Sai Tok's flat, gambled for an hour and a half before going down to a coffee stall at Block 33 for a Tiger beer. He walked back to Sai Tok's flat, used the toilet, and returned to the hawker centre for another bottle of beer. Just before he did, he saw June and Lim sitting at a stone table. He finished his drink and went to the toilet. When he came back, June and Lim were sitting at his table.

Smiling at Lim, he said, 'I'd like to have a private talk with June.'

Lim left the table.

'This is not your private spot,' she said to him. 'You have no right to ask anyone to leave.'

'June, about that day, I'm truly sorry,' he said earnestly.

'I can't forgive you,' she said. 'And I wish to have my gold chain and gold ring back.'

'But I've pawned them.'

'How could you do such a thing!' she scolded him loudly. 'They belong to me! Not you!' She got up and made a phone call while he sat there, not looking at her. When she came back he said, 'Please June, don't let people know we're quarrelling. Why don't we go to a quiet place to talk – the open space beside Block 6.'

She walked in front of him as they made their

way there. At the open space, Hok held her hand and tried to explain himself. She pulled away and began to chide him again. A woman who knew them passed by, noticed them, and said, 'Hey, anything wrong? Take it easy.'

'Let me explain, June,' he said again.

'What is there to explain,' she said. 'You've brought me shame by first insulting me and then pawning my things. If you don't return them to me, you'd better be careful.'

The last words stung him like salt on a raw wound. He found it impossible to control himself any longer, and in a blur and confused anger, he saw his own fist lunging out at her abdomen. She staggered back from the blow. As he moved up to punch her again she whipped out something in her hand and thrust it at him. As he grabbed it a stinging pain raced up his fingers. A knife. The object she had in her hand was a knife. Trying to wrench it from her, he grabbed the blade with his left hand and her free hand with his right. He pushed forward into a half-squat, and she slipped and sat on the ground. She tried to kick him, and he twisted the blade towards her legs to stop her. Then, twisting the blade towards her, he thrust it.

An instant later, she let go of the knife and clutched at her abdomen. The knife was in his hand now, and as she turned away, he stabbed her once in the back. She turned again and he stabbed the right side of her body.

Then he saw the red stains spreading on her blouse. There was no more anger now, only fear, fear that she might die. He dropped the blade. He held up

99

his right hand and saw blood. His T-shirt was splattered with spots of blood. June was trying to sit up. He looked at her for the last time.

Then he ran.

He ran across the road to an open space between Blocks 21 and 22, then to Block 24 where he stumbled up a flight of steps to the 12th storey. When he reached the landing, he vomited. Two men came out, and seeing him, offered to call the police. But Hok asked them to contact his family instead. They called, but the phone wasn't answered; he asked them to call his grandmother. They came back and said she wanted him to stay where he was. After some time, his mother came. He told her he had been involved in a fight, and she brought him to his auntie's house where she cleaned his cuts and bloodstains.

June was found a short distance from where she had been stabbed. She was immediately rushed to hospital. But her injuries were too grave, and she never made it.

It was St Valentine's Eve.

After learning that June had died, Hok surrendered himself.

SIMS AVENUE: 1.30 A.M.

THE CRIMES

26th February, 1960. Major Wedderburn was driving along Holland Road; he was bringing a payroll of $35,000 to Singapore Regiment Camp at Ulu Pandan. Suddenly, a taxi pulled up close to his car. Guns blazed. Major Wedderburn was shot in the back. He never reached the camp.

10th August, 1960. Ho Cheow Chye, 58, was an owner of Bukit Tiga Estate. At 9.00 a.m., he drove his Ford Consul from his Mawai Village home to the estate. Along Sedili Road, he saw a white and yellow Hillman car ahead of him; and he caught a glimpse of the four men inside as he overtook it. When he came to the estate, he stopped the car, got down, and handed a parcel of maize to one of his rubber-tappers.

As he was returning to his car, he saw the same Hillman parked about 12 yards behind his Ford. No one was inside. Nothing seemed to be amiss, and he got back into his car.

He didn't have a chance to turn on the ignition. Four men suddenly appeared at his side – two of them had automatics in their hands.

'Don't start the car,' one of them told Ho in Hokkien. 'And don't try to shout.' When he saw that Ho was obeying him, he said, 'Now, get out of your car and walk into the other one.' Ho went to the car and sat at the back. One of them placed cotton wool over his eyes, then made him wear a pair of glasses to secure the cotton wool. Two men sat on either side of him. Before they drove off, he heard one of them tell another to 'immobilise' his car.

The cotton wool and the spectacles didn't cut off Ho's vision entirely, and he saw the car turn into a track leading to Eng Hong timber-logging area. They travelled for a short while before the car came to a halt. Once out of the car, they removed the glasses and covered his eyes with medicinal plasters. They tied his hands and feet, then dumped him into the boot.

The car moved again for about another hour. When it finally stopped, he was carried out of the car and afterwards put on a wooden floor. Still blind-folded, he remained where he was. None of them spoke to him. Later, he was given some rice and meat.

Several hours later, he was driven again to another destination. Ho was released unhurt a few days later after his wife paid a ransom of $60,000.

This was only one of twelve kidnappings that occurred between 12th October, 1959 and 22nd August, 1960. Victims included some wealthy tow-kays. The total amount of ransom money paid to the kidnappers was $740,000.

THE INVESTIGATION

After intensive investigation, police discovered a thread that connected the 12 kidnappings and the murder of Major Wedderburn. Oh Kim Kee, a 29-year-old notorious underworld figure, was believed to have participated in most if not all of these crimes. He was a member of the 24 Secret Society operating in Sembawang. In 1954, he was arrested for an armed robbery and sentenced to eight years' imprisonment. But he was released four years later because they had found him to be a 'model prisoner'.

Back in the streets again, he began to organise criminal activities. Oh had a partner in crime, Yang Nan Yang, who was a member of the 969 S.S. operating at Weld Road and Sungei Road. In 1954, Yang had been placed on two years' probation, and in '58, he was charged and acquitted for possession of firearms. After several successful kidnappings, Oh Kim Kee became the man the rich feared.

THE TIP-OFF

For a long time, Oh Kim Kee had artfully dodged the law. Police had failed to pin him down not only because he was clever, but also because the kidnapped victims didn't give the necessary cooperation.

Police combed the entire island, searching, enquiring. It took them months. Then, on 23rd August, 1960, a day after the last victim was kidnapped, Inspector Loh Poh Cheng of the Cantonese section, CID, was informed that Oh and Yang Nan Yang were holed up in an old flat at Sims Avenue. Oh would be sleeping at the front of the flat while Yang the back. Inspector Loh was also told that if they were in, their cars would be parked below the flat: Oh's was a Mercedes SB 7852 and Yang's was a Hillman SU 2228. Loh was also warned that Oh had guns with him which he would not hesitate to use.

THE PLAN

Loh relayed the information to Acting Superintendent Ong Kian Tong who then summoned a team of twelve CID officers. It was 12.30 a.m. on 24th August, 1960. Surrounded by detectives, and with the help of the flat's plan, Ong Kian Tong planned the raid.

Ag DSP Lim Chye Heng, Ag ASP Ng Leng Hua, Insps T Perreau and Chia Cheng Poh formed the first party. 'The four of you,' Ong said, 'will take positions at the back lane. You are to cover the spiral staircase leading from the back of the flat. When you find the coast clear, approach the flat by way of the stairs.'

'Insp Nadarajah and Det Ho,' Ong said to the second party, 'you will cover the ground floor in front.'

'DSP Ratnasingam, Insps Samuel, Loh, Chan, Lian and I will go in from the front,' Ong said. 'If we go there and find the cars not around, we'll set an ambush for them. If the cars are there, and we assume Oh and Yang are inside, we split into two the moment we enter. Lian, Chan and I will take room A, the rest of you take room D. There'll be a troop of the Reserve Unit to cordon off the entire block once we give the signal that the men are in.'

Ong looked at his men and saw they understood the plan. 'Let's go,' he said.

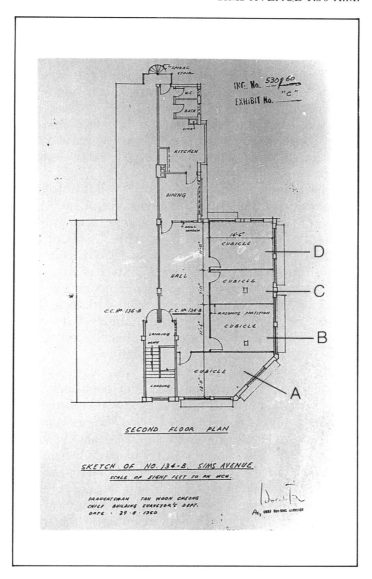

ING. No. 530 60

EXHIBIT No. "C"

SECOND FLOOR PLAN

SKETCH OF NO. 134-B. SIMS AVENUE.
SCALE OF EIGHT FEET TO AN INCH.

DRAUGHTSMAN TAN WOON CHEONG
CHIEF BUILDING SURVEYOR'S DEPT.
DATE 29·8·1960

THE SIEGE

The flat was on the top floor of a three-storey building at Sims Avenue, Geylang. A coffee stall took up a large part of the ground floor, and the back of the building was surrounded by an eight-foot wall topped with a fence.

Sims Avenue was asleep when the police arrived. Except for several cars that were parked around the building, the street lamps shone weakly on the empty streets.

The criminals' cars were there. A collapsible gate and a wooden door barred the entrance of the front stairs. The gate was secured by a spring lock, and the door by a Yale. Both were toys at the hands of the criminal hunters. But the door was locked from the inside, too. Insp Lian then prised off a door panel with a crowbar, leaving just enough space for one man to go through at a time. In semi-darkness, Ong and his party got through in three minutes. But in the process, considerable noise was created, and they could hear movements inside the flat.

In the flat itself, Yang Nang Yang was aroused from his sleep by a banging from the front door. He got up, and unbolting the door, saw Oh Kim Kee running from his room to the kitchen. Yang went to the back of the room and looked out the rear window. He saw a police riot van parked nearby. Policemen were scuttling around the building. He decided to come out of his room to take a peep through the eyepiece of the front door. As he walked across the hall, he saw a wide opening in the front door and men coming through it. He ran into the chief tenant's room (room C).

Insp Chan entered the flat first. He passed through the opening, and as he made a dash into room A, his eyes picked out a dark form crouching at the door of room D. Once inside room A, he switched on the lights, and at the same moment, an explosion from a gun shattered the silence. Insp Lian was just entering the flat and the bullet whistled past him and bit into a partition two feet from where Chan stood. Lian dove for cover behind a chair.

Chan took a quick peep at the figure again. It had a pistol in each hand. Lian then ran to join Chan.

Ong, Ratnasingam and Loh burst into the flat. Ratnasingam and Loh saw the figure at the door, Ong didn't. He had been told that Oh kept his firearms in room D, and not knowing the gunman was crouching by its doorway, he scrambled towards the room.

A shot, followed by another, rang out. The bullets took him in both arms. Groaning in pain, he turned and dashed into room C. Yang, the chief tenant and his two children were crouching at a corner of the room. Seconds later, Yang's wife ran out of room D and came in to join him.

Ratnasingam, Loh and Samuel then decided to make a run for the dining room – from the dining room, they could cover the rear of room D as well as unlock the rear door for party 1, led by Lim Chye Heng, to enter. As they ran for it, they passed the doorway of room D, and Loh squeezed off four shots into D's doorway. One bullet pinged into the gunman's thigh.

In the dining room, Samuel went to the rear door and admitted the first party. When he came back, he, Lim Chye Heng and Ratnasingam fired from the window at a moving shape in room D. The man in the room retaliated with two shots.

Ratnasingam sent Lim Chye Heng down to request for help from the Reserve Unit which was stationed on the road below. ASP Bridges, heading the unit, fired five rounds of Flite Rite teargas shells and three long range shells from a pavement of an opposite building. The shells landed neatly in the room.

The police waited for about twenty minutes for the teargas to take effect. Lim then asked the gunman to surrender through a loud hailer. The gunman didn't answer, but that moment offered Ong the opportunity to get out of the room. Afraid that Yang might either take advantage of his injury or dash into room D to join the gunman, Ong quickly took the occupants out of room C. No shots were fired as they emerged. Ong and the women were taken to hospital while Yang was held in custody.

AC CID, Cheah Teng Cheoh arrived at 2.10 a.m. He sent Ong and the women to hospital, then came back. With an Inspector of the Reserve Unit, he threaded up the front stairs. From the entrance, he fired shells of teargas at the room. The shells went off target, bounced off the wall and landed in the hall, smoking.

Cheah called out several times to the gunman, 'You are surrounded! Surrender now!'

No response.

Lim and Bridges came in by the spiral staircase carrying Stirling guns. Positioning himself at the dining room window, Bridges squeezed off several rounds into the gunman's room. Lim fired a teargas shell into the room, then borrowed a rifle from a Reserve Unit constable and fired two rounds. After that, he asked for his Stirling gun, and from the hall, sprayed bullets into room D.

A groaning began from the room, but the gunman still refused to submit himself. Minutes later, the detectives decided to move in.

An attack was planned: Loh was to quickly open the door and remove the curtain so that Lim, with the Stirling gun, could fire inside.

Lim loaded a new magazine into his Stirling. When he was ready, he looked at Loh and nodded.

In one quick, fluid motion, Loh ran up to the room, kicked the door open, tore the curtain aside. Lim followed up, kneeling by the doorway, gun poised.

A fusillade of gunfire echoed through the entire flat. The Stirling spat thirty rounds into the dark, and when he stopped firing, Lim held up an Aldis lamp and saw the gunman under the bed. He was lying in a puddle of his own blood, groaning, still clutching a revolver in each hand. Lim went up to the man, and taking away the revolvers, recognised him to be Oh Kim Kee.

The hunt was over.

No. 1 THUG KILLED

'They'll never get me alive' was boast of Public Enemy No. 1, killed in hail of shots

An official after-death picture of Oh Kim Kee – Public Enemy No. 1.

The final shoot-out. The desperate gunman took cover under a bed but did not manage to survive.

EPILOGUE

A crowd had gathered around the building, and the police had to cordon them off.

Oh was taken to hospital by an ambulance. He died on arrival. He had in his pockets a fifty-dollar note and ninety-six ten-dollar notes. He was wearing a watch taken from one of the kidnapped victims.

Post mortem revealed that twelve bullets hit Oh, all from the front. Three bullets were extracted from the body and examined. One was found to be from Loh Poh Cheng's gun, and the other two from the Stirling fired by Lim Chye Heng.

111

Arrow points to a trap door leading to the underground cell in which at least four kidnapped towkays are believed to have been held captive.

The house in Jalan Kemaan, Johore Bahru, where kidnapper Oh Kim Kee held victims in an underground cell until ransom money was paid. Police found the address of the house in Oh's Sims Avenue flat after he was killed. The arrow points to an opening leading to the cell.

A search of the flat was carried out and among the items found were a third revolver, fully loaded, five extra rounds, a dagger, and a wirecutter.

These findings, together with the capture of Nan Yang, helped police solve 7 out of 12 kidnapping cases, detaining in the process 11 other people, and recovering some of the ransom money. Police also discovered a bungalow at Jalan Kemaan and a flat at Jalan Abdul Samad, both in Johore, where Oh had kept his victims.

The Minister for Home Affairs, Mr Ong Pang Boon, sent his congratulations to the lawmen for having done an excellent job; and for the next few days, the newspapers gave a full coverage of the Sims Avenue drama, complete with photographs. According to one, the 25th August 1960 edition of *The Singapore Free Press*, Oh Kim Kee had once boasted, 'They'll never get me alive.'

He was right.

THE CHARTERED BANK ROBBERY

John Graham was a sergeant attached to the Royal New Zealand Air Force. On Wednesday, 19th March, 1980, he brought his daughter, Cindy, 4, to Chartered Bank, Hillview Road. He visited the bank at least twice a month. The bank, a one-storey building, stood alone on a raised plot. Around it, royal palms, Croton and Acalaypha grew on planted cow grass. A short flight of steps and a cement passage, sheltered above and open to the surroundings at the sides led to the main entrance of the bank. On a wall of the bank the blue logo and blue Chinese characters obscured the words 'Chartered Bank' which was in white.

John drove; he reached the place at 2.15 p.m., and parked his car. Walking towards the bank with his daughter, he saw three Malays approaching the bank, too. He went in, took out his account booklet, and began to fill in a withdrawal form.

Yew May Lee, a bank clerk, was working in the cash room enclosed by wooden frames with glass panels. Looi Peng Nam, a cashier, was speaking with general clerk, Lee Wing Locke. Lim Bock Chua, another bank clerk, was conversing on the phone. Lee Chee Seng, machine operator, was clearing cheques with his machine. Salatoon bin Samood, bank security, stood at the bank's inner office. Several other bank staff and visitors were actively transacting: cheque for money, money for drafts, withdrawing, saving. It seemed an ordinary, business-filled afternoon.

After filling his form, John Graham handed it to the clerk at the counter, and at the same moment, an explosion rocked the entire room. Wing Locke felt a pain at his neck, and reaching up with his fingers, felt the wet redness of blood. When John looked up he saw that the people behind the counter had both hands raised. A man, faceless beneath a translucent stocking, pointed a revolver at the bank staff. Salatoon reached for his service revolver, a .38 Smith and Wesson, but the sight of a nasty barrel stopped him. The gunman ordered him to lie down. He did as told, knowing it would be foolish to resist. The gunman took away his weapon. Two other men, faces also hidden in stockings, came in. One of them shouted, 'Don't move!'. His hand held a revolver.

John pushed Cindy towards the wall, using himself as a shield. His back to Cindy, he raised his hands, keeping his head down and looking back at her to make sure that she was safe. Then, someone shouted, 'Get down!' and he sank onto his knees.

When John turned his head to look in front again, he saw that the one who had fired the shot now had two revolvers in his hand, brandishing them like a gunfighter in the old West. 'Hands up!' he shouted, leaping onto the counter. 'We don't want to hurt you. We just want your money!'

Salatoon stole a glance at the shooter. He saw Salatoon looking and pinned a shot at him, missing him by inches.

'Money, money! More money!' the shooter shouted, standing guard on the counter.

One accomplice went over to the drawers and began taking the loot. Another who was guarding the entrance with a gun ran over, jumped on and over the counter. Peng Nam, prone on the floor by then, saw him come down. The robber tried in vain to open the cashier's drawer because the key had to be turned a little before it could open. He pointed the revolver at Peng Nam. 'Open it! Open it!' he said. Peng Nam obeyed. The man scooped the dollar bills from the drawer into a blue and yellow bag.

In less than five minutes, the robbers were already on their way out. A parting shot rang out, and the shooter yelled, 'Thank you!'

The robbers escaped in a blue Toyota Corolla parked along Hillview Avenue. They had done well. They pulled off a daring robbery in broad daylight and walked away with $37,931/-.

Detective Jaswinder Singh of the Organised Crime Branch, CID, decided to pay G H Niteclub at Battery Road a visit. He had been told that only a few days before, one of the boys there had been showing a gun around, and Jaswinder smelled something in the air. Positioning himself at the counter, he waited for the suspect to turn up. At 12.15 a.m. in the morning, Jaswinder's 'casual' source informed him that the suspect, a man who he thought was one of the Chartered Bank armed robbers, had just arrived. One of the nightclub captains had sat down with him. Jaswinder went to his car, got his handcuffs, returned to the nightclub. He approached the man.

'Jaswinder Singh, CID,' he said, catching the suspect with both hands. 'Let's go to the office.' He looked at the captain. 'You, too.'

In the office he handcuffed the suspect and the captain, then frisked them. Nothing but $407/- in cash.

'Who are you? What do you do for a living?' he asked the suspect.

'I am a handyman,' the suspect replied. 'I get $200/- a month.'

'Then how come you have so much money?'

'I won it at the races,' the man answered unsteadily, beginning to sweat.

'What about the gun you were showing around the other day?'

'Oh, that's a toy gun,' he said. 'I have thrown it in the canal at Bukit Timah.'

Jaswinder then called Inspector Colin Choo, the officer-in-charge. Colin was at the nightclub in 25 minutes. Suspecting that the rest of the robbers would be meeting this one soon, they laid an ambush. An hour later, none of them turned up. The police officers left with their suspect. He was Kamsari bin Jumadi. At the station at 2.00 in the morning, Colin Choo interrogated Kamsari, and at 5.40 a.m., had Jaswinder lock up the suspect. That same morning at about 6.55 a.m., he interrogated Kamsari again. This time, the suspect admitted being somehow involved in the Chartered Bank robbery. He ceased questioning and instructed DPC Lee Lai Heng to escort the suspect to Changi Prison Hospital for a medical examination.

At 2.50 the next morning, Kamsari led a party of detectives to a house in Lorong Lompang. He told them that the revolvers, kept by Mohd Salleh bin Abdullah, were in the house. The lawmen raided the house and arrested Mohd Salleh bin Abdullah who surrendered 3 revolvers and some ammunition.

They were:

1. A .38 Smith and Wesson special, serial number: 'Cisco 49'. It was wrapped in a piece of cloth together with one live round and hidden in a crevice of a room.
2. An empty .22 Ruby revolver.
3. A .38 Colt with one round in the 6 o'clock chamber.
4. Four .22 rounds and three .38 rounds. These were found in a playing card box which was inside a plastic bag.

Money amounting to $6,400/- was recovered from Salleh's cupboard.

Salleh bin Abdullah had participated in the robbery as the driver of the Corolla. A little more than an hour later, the detectives were led to Hishamrudin's house at Lily Avenue. They searched the house, but found nothing. They then went to an empty room at Chua Chu Kang Road where they recovered three .38 Special spent cartridge casings. Kamsari pointed to a yellow plastic bag which was used by Hishamrudin in the robbery.

The two suspects were taken to court and they were left in police custody for a week.

From the suspects and other sources, police gathered that there were more people involved besides Hishamrudin: Ameran bin Mohd Salleh (son of the driver in the robbery) did not participate directly in the robbery, but the revolvers used, the Colt and the Ruby, belonged to him; and Mohd Salleh bin Awang, the one who did all the shooting during the robbery.

Police found out that Hishamrudin and Ameran had been arrested by the Malaysian police and were detained in Kelantan. The Malaysian police had acted on the request of the Singapore police to arrest both of them. So on 25th March, 1980, six days after the robbery, Inspector Chua Sok Meng and detectives Jaswinder Singh, Dolak Singh and Lee Yang Ann, armed with warrants from the subordinate court, took a train up to Kelantan where they took over the custody of Ameran and Hishamrudin. On the way back, the two captives gave statements to the police.

Mohd Salleh bin Awang, the leader of the gang, remained at large.

Kamsari described to the police how the Chartered Bank robbery was planned:

Mohd Salleh bin Awang, the shooter, had called him on the phone at 3.00 p.m. on 16th March, 1980, a week before the robbery.

'Kamsari? Salleh here. Come over to Lorong Lompang now. Get Hishamrudin to come along, too.'

In an hour and a half, Kamsari and Hishamrudin

20 Lorong Lompang.

reached their destination. Kamsari waited while Hishamrudin walked over to Salleh's house to call him. When Hishamrudin returned with Salleh, they began to discuss the robbery. The three had committed robberies before, and successfully at that; this was just going to be another heist.

'Chartered Bank at Upper Bukit Timah Road is a good place,' Salleh bin Awang said. 'We strike tomorrow.'

At 10.00 p.m. that same day, after the three had

broken up and gone home, Salleh called Kamsari again.

'About the robbery,' he said to Kamsari, 'it's off. I can't get the transport for our escape. Meet me tomorrow at the same place.'

At 3.00 the next afternoon, the three met at Lorong Lompang again. Salleh bin Awang did most of the talking. 'I've got a man to drive us in our getaway,' he said. 'He will park the car outside the bank, along Hillview Avenue. We'd have to take a bus there, rush into the bank, rob, and hurry into the car.'

The discussion lasted only fifteen minutes, after which Kamsari and Hishamrudin took a bus home and S. bin Awang returned to S. bin Abdullah's house.

On the 18th, the three met at Hishamrudin's place. The plan the day before had been sketchy, and they now discussed it in detail. Salleh bin Awang had a white plastic bag before them. Opening it, he showed the .38 Colt and the .22 Ruby which Kamsari had used nine days before: the three of them were walking along Battery Road towards G H Niteclub when they came upon a group of Malay men arguing over a woman. Salleh bin Awang told the other two to break the group up. Kamsari masqueraded as a police officer and ordered the group to cease their argument. To convince them he wasn't bluffing, he pulled out the Ruby which Salleh bin Awang had handed to him earlier, holding it in such a way that the crowd could see what it was – that's how Jaswinder Singh's source came to know about the gun. The sight of the Ruby broke the crowd up. Later,

Kamsari gave the revolver back to Salleh bin Awang.

'Clean these,' the leader said. 'Make sure you get the oil off.' After cleaning the revolvers, they handed them to Salleh bin Awang who wrapped them up in the plastic bag and pushed the bag under Hishamrudin's bed. They started drinking Guinness Stout, and as they did so Salleh bin Awang took a piece of paper and sketched the plan.

'Tomorrow, after lunch, we leave here by bus. When we reach Hillview Avenue, we alight and walk towards the bank. There, I'll give you the signal to enter. "Uncle" (Salleh bin Abdullah) will be waiting in a car outside the bank.' He took a swig before continuing. 'Kamsari, you'll use the Ruby to guard the main entrance. Hishamrudin, your job is to get the cash. Don't waste time. Take it as fast as possible. I'll take care of the Cisco guard on duty inside the bank.'

Around ten in the morning, they awoke, bathed and had breakfast, and acted normally so that Hishamrudin's family members didn't suspect anything unusual about them. At noon, Kamsari went back to his own house to look for a knife which Salleh bin Awang had asked him to procure for Hishamrudin. When he came back less than an hour later, Salleh bin Awang had him go to the shop to buy two bottles of Guinness Stout. He got the stout, and back at Hishamrudin's house, they rehearsed their parts in the robbery: Salleh bin Awang once again drew a sketch of the bank's plan and instructed the other two what they were supposed to do. While he was talking, Kamsari asked, 'How do you know the layout of the bank?'

'I've been there. I've surveyed the place,' S. bin Awang replied.

'There is one thing I want to make clear,' Kamsari said. 'Our aim is to rob the bank of cash. We must not shoot anyone during the robbery.'

'Okay,' Salleh bin Awang said. 'But I can't promise you I won't use the gun if I'm forced to.'

He handed the .22 Ruby and five live rounds to Kamsari. The Colt was to be used by Salleh bin Awang himself. Hishamrudin was handed the scout knife. Loading the rounds into the .22, Kamsari accidentally squeezed off a round. The bullet ploughed into the floor. Luckily though, the report was drowned out by the high volume of the radio, and no one outside the room heard.

Salleh bin Awang scolded Kamsari for his carelessness. Kamsari, frightened by the roar of the gun, told Salleh bin Awang to forget the robbery.

'Sorry, but we have to go through with it,' Salleh bin Awang said. 'I've already informed Salleh Abdullah that it is to take place today.'

2.00 p.m.: the three of them left Hishamrudin's house. A bus brought them to Bukit Timah Road in ten minutes. They walked to a telephone booth to await the arrival of the getaway car. When it came, Salleh bin Awang instructed them to make for the bank: Kamsari walked ahead, followed by Hishamrudin, then S. bin Awang. Kamsari had the .22 tucked in his pants at the waist. Salleh bin Awang had stuffed the .38 in his right hip pocket. On the way there, they saw a Caucasian male (John Graham) in uniform getting out of his car. Kamsari saw him looking at them.

'Salleh,' he said. 'Let's forget it.'

'Listen,' the leader replied. 'We've come this far. Don't spoil it now!' They watched John Graham and his daughter enter the bank. Then the leader instructed, 'Put on your masks.'

Salleh bin Awang rushed into the bank. Hishamrudin followed. And as Kamsari entered, the first shot rang out . . .

They rushed out with the loot and headed for the getaway car which had its engine running. Salleh bin Awang sat in front, the others at the back. As the car drove off, they pulled the stockings off. Salleh bin Abdullah headed along Hillview Avenue, made a left turn to Jurong Road. In the car, Salleh bin Awang instructed him to drive to Lorong Sensuai. When they reached Sensuai, the three men got down. 'Drive to your house,' the leader told the driver. 'Leave the car there, then join us at 541-C Chua Chu Kang Road.' The three of them walked through a kampung before coming to a bus stop at Upper Bukit Timah Road, the place from which they had just escaped. They boarded a 172 which would bring them all the way back to Chua Chu Kang, where Salleh bin Awang had rented a room. As the bus was nearing Bukit Panjang Circus, Kamsari noticed a police road block ahead. In spite of being very nervous, for he still had the revolver with him, he appeared calm, and the bus was let through without a search.

At Chua Chu Kang, they alighted and walked to the room which Salleh bin Awang had rented. The loot was divided equally and each pocketed about $7,200/-. The balance was given to Salleh bin

Abdullah for having procured the revolvers (later, Ameran, Salleh bin Abdullah's son, had demanded a share of the loot by insisting that the revolvers were his) and used to pay up some of Salleh bin Awang's debts. Some money was then set aside to pay for the car which Salleh bin Abdullah had hired from Johore Bahru, as well as for a *kenduri* (feast) to celebrate their success.

After splitting the loot, Salleh bin Awang told Salleh bin Abdullah to keep the three guns and the remaining rounds of ammunition. And the next day, 20th March, 1980, the *kenduri* was held at Salleh bin Abdullah's place. Less than a week later, all of them except Salleh bin Awang were hauled in by the net of the law.

Kamsari was sentenced to life imprisonment and 6 strokes of the cane.

Salleh bin Abdullah was sentenced to 10 years' imprisonment.

Hishamrudin bin Mohamed Sham was sentenced to 10 years' imprisonment and 6 strokes of the cane.

Ameran bin Mohamed Salleh, in spite of not being involved in the Chartered Bank Robbery, was sentenced to 12 years' imprisonment and 10 strokes of the cane for consorting with Salleh bin Awang who carried a firearm when they robbed an A & W Restaurant at Floral Mile, Bukit Timah Road; and a money changer at Clifford Pier.

The leader and mastermind, Salleh bin Awang escaped. That same year, in an attempted robbery, he murdered a New Zealand army sergeant, Arthur James Yaxley, at a beach resort in Johore. He was finally apprehended by the Malaysian police, sentenced to death on 28th March, 1982, and executed on 27th April, 1985.

* * * * * * * * * * * * * * * *

BY PERSONS UNKNOWN

The date was 29th August, 1979. Wai Lin, a servant in the employ of the Lim family, came to work at 9.30 a.m., the usual time. She had been working for the Lims for about six years. Every day, she did the chores – including marketing – till 3.30 in the afternoon, went back to her own home, and returned at 5.30 to prepare dinner for the family. At 8.30 p.m., she'd leave after washing up.

On this day, she entered the main gate which was closed but unlocked. She used her own key to let herself in. After putting the morning's marketing in the kitchen, she went upstairs and saw that Lian Choo, 14, was sleeping in her room. No one else was at home. She walked over to the girl and tapped her lightly. 'Lian Choo, Lian Choo,' she asked. 'Why aren't you in school?'

'I'm not feeling well,' Lian Choo replied drowsily. In fact, after dinner the night before, Lian Choo had already begun to feel unwell.

'Are you hungry?' she asked Lian Choo.

'Yes. Could you cook some Kuay Teow for me?'

'All right. Go back to sleep. I'll call you when the food's ready.'

Wai Lin went about her chores first, then cooked the Kuay Teow. When she had finished cooking she carried the bowl of Kuay Teow up to Lian Choo's bedroom.

'Lian Choo,' she said, waking the girl up the second time. 'Your food is ready.'

The girl sat up, took the steaming bowl from the servant, and asked, 'Wai Lin, could you buy some sweets and Sng Moi for me?'

'All right,' Wai Lin said, and went to the shop opposite the house and bought twenty cents worth of the 'Sng Moi' and four Hacks sweets for the girl. After giving Lian Choo the titbits, she resumed her housework. At 3.30, she went upstairs to Lian Choo's room. 'I'm going home now,' she told the girl. 'Don't open the door for strangers.' With that, Wai Lin returned home.

That was the last time anyone saw Lim Lian Choo alive. Around six the next morning, fifteen hours and thirty minutes after Wai Lin left her, a Commando Battalion, having completed their sectional proficiency test at Sime Road and about to return to camp, spotted a charred, blackened female body. Later, it was identified as Lian Choo's. She was clad in dark blue shorts and what remained of a burnt T-shirt, the same attire in which Wai Lin had last seen her.

She had no footwear on.

And she was 14 km away from her home.

* Sng Moi is a dried, salty and sour preserved fruit.

The road leading to the mud track, about 100 m to the left.

Lian Choo's death came as a shock to her family, particularly her father, whom she was very dear to.

Lian Choo was the youngest child in a family of two boys and two girls. After her mother died, her father became acquainted with another woman, Lily Choy. Choy came to the house often, and the children called her 'auntie'. Choy then began to stay at the Lim residence and Lian Choo told a friend that she feared her father would stop loving her now that he had found another woman.

Choy and Lian Choo became quite close: Choy also brought her to her own home, which she liked to visit.

On 27th August, two days before Lian Choo's death, Lim had told her he was going to Kuala Lumpur on business, and Lian Choo's last words to him were, 'Papa, I hope you will come back as soon as your job in Malaysia is over.'

The next day, 28th August, Lim drove to Malaysia. That evening, Lian Choo complained of a headache and Wai Lin prepared some herbal tea for her; before leaving, she asked Choy, who was also in the house, to see that the girl slept. Wai Lin left the house. Choy stayed with Lian Choo till she fell asleep, which was past 11.30 p.m., then Choy went back to her own home. She didn't stay because she had to attend to her own daughters.

The next afternoon, the 29th, Lily Choy was at her home when Lian Choo called. It was about 3.30, shortly after Wai Lin had left.

'Auntie, I'm going out with friends,' Lian Choo told her.

'You shouldn't,' Choy advised. 'You're ill.'

'But I want to go,' Lian Choo had said.

'Wait there,' Choy said. 'I'm coming over now.'

But Lian Choo had already hung up.

Choy immediately drove to the Lim residence; she arrived half an hour later. The gates weren't locked, but the door to the house was. Choy did not have the key to the door so she called Lian Choo from outside. No one answered. She called again; still there was no reply. Assuming the girl might be asleep, she drove to a shop nearby and called the house, letting the phone ring for a long time. The receiver at the

131

other end was never picked up. Choy went home and called again at 7.30 that night. Someone answered, but it was only Wai Lin, the servant.

'How is Lian Choo?' Choy asked.

'She's not in,' Wai Lin said. 'I think she's gone out with her friends.'

Choy decided to go back to the house.

Lian Choo's eldest brother returned home at 8.30 p.m. Wai Lin told him Lian Choo had gone out but he assured her there was nothing to worry about and that she could return home.

The morning on which Lian Choo's body was found, Choy went to Lian Choo's school to see if she was there. She wasn't. The principal and teacher advised her to call the police but she didn't know how. That afternoon, family members began calling Lian Choo's friends. None of them knew anything of her disappearance.

On the afternoon of 31st August, Lim came back to Singapore. His second son, Boon Heng, informed him that Lian Choo had been missing for the past two days. Boon Cheng, the other son, read in the papers about a burnt body found off Sime Road and reported the case to the police, showing them a photograph of his sister. He was brought to see the body, and identified it as Lian Choo's.

Meanwhile, at the Lim residence, Choy suggested they look for any note that Lian Choo could have left behind. Lian Gek searched her sister's room, and found a suicide note in her cupboard. The note, written in Mandarin, was addressed to her father.

Here is the police translation of the note:

Father,

I, your unfilial daughter, got acquainted with a man last year. In the beginning, we met once weekly or biweekly. Four months later, we were getting more fond of each other. Last month we decided to get engaged secretly at the end of this year and then have our marriage solemnized when I have completed my secondary four education.

However, to my surprise, he suddenly rang me up on this Monday afternoon and told me that he incidentally befriended a new girl last week. She is not only pretty but also sociable. He further added that she was from a wealthy family. According to what he said, his girl friend is better than I in every aspect. He never realised that by so doing, he had broken my heart.

Other than that, he also said something cruel. On hearing that, I really wanted to slap him and also reproach him for being a heartless playboy. However, I realised that there was no point in arguing with such a mean person. Furthermore, the matter had reached such a stage, what can I do? I really cannot stand such a blow. At times, I asked myself: What does life mean to me? I concluded that it was better to die.

Father, I feel very guilty to you, for you have brought me up with much painstaking efforts. For the past ten over years, you have shed blood and sweat because of me. However, I really cannot control myself. As such, the only way to release me from my sorrow and trouble is to kill myself. Your kindness for bringing me up can only be repaid in the next life. I beg you to forgive this unfilial daughter.

From a most unfilial daughter

==

Undated. Unsigned.

At the scene of death, the mud track off Sime Road, which was a dumping ground, police discovered several things:

1. Two match sticks with only the heads burnt 2 metres away from the body, and a box of matches about 4 metres away.
2. A tin bearing the label 'Shell Rotella' oil, containing some brownish liquid, 10 metres from the body.
3. A pair of gloves near the body.
4. The deceased had no footwear on, nor was any footwear found in the vicinity.

The Department of Scientific Services tested these articles and came up with the following conclusions:

i.   There was no trace of kerosene or petrol on the matchbox or matches or the gloves.
ii. The brownish liquid in the can was of low volatility, and could hardly be used as a combustible fuel.

The forensic pathologist, on performing the autopsy, discovered that:

1. The death was caused by severe burns, and the fuel used was kerosene.
2. The deceased was a non-virgin, but had not been sexually assaulted, nor did she suffer any internal abnormality or injury.
3. There were fine soot particles found in the larynx.
4. The time of death was about 10.00 p.m. (29th August).

5. The Document Examiner confirmed that the handwriting on the suicide note belonged to the deceased.

According to Lian Choo's family members:
1. Whenever she went out, she wore either long pants or skirt, never a pair of shorts.
2. Her pair of spectacles were in her drawer.
3. The main door was locked when Wai Lin returned at 5.30 p.m. on the afternoon of Lian Choo's disappearance.
4. Her brother Boon Heng had received 4 phone calls from a man who seemed to be about 18 years old.

With the facts at hand, what conclusions can we draw? Was it SUICIDE? Or MURDER?

Suppose all that the note stated was true, that Lian Choo did get involved with an unknown man, that they had something going between them and that he did call her up Monday, 28th August, to tell her they were through. That could account for her feeling unwell that night. The next afternoon, after the servant had left, she could have taken a cab to Sime Road, buying some kerosene and matches on the way, and taken her own life. Knowing that she was going to die, she didn't bother to put on proper clothes.

Possible, but highly unlikely. For instance, why didn't she place the suicide note where her father or someone else could easily find it? And why go all the way to the track off Sime Road, 14 km from her home? How could she have drenched herself with kerosene, lighted herself, and then thrown the matches and box aside – without getting kerosene on the box or the matches? And why wasn't the kerosene container found anywhere near the body?

Now, assuming that she was murdered, this is what MIGHT have happened: She got emotionally and physically involved with this mystery man. When he did call her that night to tell her he was through with her, she became despondent, hence unwell. She might have decided to take her own life, but after having written the note, changed her mind and put it in her drawer; because if she really intended to, it's more likely she'd have placed it in her father's room, in his drawer or cupboard, or even in the living room where someone could have found it easily. The next afternoon, when the servant had left, this unknown man might have come in a car to see her, before which he gave her a call and told her he wanted to talk things over (accounting for her phoning Choy up and insisting she wanted to go out with friends). The man came, went into her house, overpowered her and forced her into the car – accounting for her not having shoes on and the fact that her shoes were missing; then drove all the way to Sime Road, murdered her (she could have been burnt and still lingered till 10.00 p.m. before expiring), and took the kerosene container with him. The two matches and matchbox were PLANTED there to make it look as though it were a suicide. Reason for murder: he thought she would expose him, and it would be worse if she had been pregnant.

If there were such a man, who was he? Why is it that nobody, not even the friends and classmates of the deceased, had ever seen him?

The coroner returned an open verdict.

Another murder, somewhat similar to the above, occurred earlier that year, this time to a middle-aged man.

THE PEPYS ROAD MURDER

In the afternoon of 10th February, 1979, Kanaga-savel, standing at the rear verandah of his house at Pepys Road, saw smoke rising from the bushes nearby. Thinking it was only a small fire that would burn itself out in time, he went back into his house and watched television. Half an hour later, a crackling noise distracted him. He looked out the window. The fire had grown enormously and was now raging in the bushes. Kanagasavel called the Fire Brigade.

Chia Eng Yong, Junior Section Leader No. 37 attached to the Central Fire Station was summoned by Control to put out a fire at Pepys Road. He and his team of firemen sped to the scene. At Eng Yong's instructions, the firemen went to work. As he battled the flames, Eng Yong spotted something black in the lallang. He went closer to inspect, and discovered that the black thing was the corpse of a man, decomposed and partially scorched. Maggots wriggled all over it.

Eng Yong reported his find to Control, which told him to inform the police.

Ho Juan Mui was a woman constable, and a former neighbour of the Fongs. Earlier, she had read

The burnt corpse was found in these bushes at Pepys Road, off Pasir Panjang.

in the Chinese papers of the disappearance of Mr Fong Tee Kik, and on 13th February, when the *Sin Chew Jit Poh* reported that a body of a decomposed man had been discovered, further describing that it was about 5 feet 6 inches with short, grey hair, she suspected that it could be her neighbour. She sought the inspector in charge of the case, Cheok Koon Seng. Cheok, after speaking with Ho, asked her to contact Fong's wife.

Inspector Cheok brought Ho and Mrs Fong to the Singapore General Hospital Mortuary. Mrs Fong was then shown some burnt clothes, shoes, socks, and belt. She identified them as belonging to her husband. And after a positive fingerprint identification, in which the thumb print from the missing man's passport was found to match that of the dead man, the body was returned to Mrs Fong.

According to Mrs Fong, her husband Fong Tee Kik, 56, had been a sailor. He had returned home from sailing in the middle of October the year before, and didn't sail again because his contract had expired.

After dinner on Friday, Mr and Mrs Fong left the house to see her godson. Mr Fong wasn't happy about his wife having adopted a godson, and on the way, they had a little misunderstanding over it. They were at Sims Avenue at that time, and Mrs Fong, deciding to cancel the visit, boarded a bus to go home. But when she was in the bus, she saw that he was still at the bus stop.

When she reached home, she told her son Leong Poo of the matter and he decided to look for him at the bus stop at Jalan Eunos, where he expected his father would alight. He waited for half an hour but when Fong didn't show up, he went home. He changed to a new set of clothes, then went to look for his father at the Sims Avenue bus stop, where his mother had left him. This time, he found the old man. On their way home, Fong said to his son, 'I'm not happy mother had adopted this godson. Ever since she did, we've been having bad luck.'

That night, and the night after, Fong slept out in the hall instead of in his own bedroom with his wife.

On 4th February, just before sunrise, some noises roused Mrs Fong from her sleep; she did not get up from bed, but saw that her husband was praying. When he had finished, he came into the room and took his shirt and trousers. The shirt was a light green, checked short-sleeves and the trousers a dark grey long pants. Without leaving word to his wife as to where he was going, Mr Fong left the house. When he failed to return home that day, his family members made calls to friends, relatives, hospitals and even the police. No one knew what had happened to him. They then published a 'Missing Person' advertisement in the Chinese newspapers, hoping that someone might have seen him.

According to Fong's wife, he had left his house without bringing his watch or wallet along. But she added that it wasn't an unusual thing for him to do. Besides, whenever Fong was angry with his wife, he would invariably sleep in the hall, and did not make a habit of telling her where he was going. As far as his son knew, Fong had no enemies. Police enquired at Offshore Logistic Far East (Pte) Ltd. where he was employed and gathered that the deceased was the 2nd engineer of Motor Vessel *Ariel* which was then being docked at Loyang Base for repairs. Fong, the personnel manager said, was a reserved man who had no quarrel with anyone on board the ship. Fong, too, was not insured.

At the scene of the crime, police found that under the body was a partially burnt Chinese paper, the *Sin Chew Jit Poh*, dated 4th February, 1979; and beside the body, an empty bottle. A search of the area revealed nothing substantial. Police then made enquiries of several people living around the area. NO ONE HAD SEEN THE DECEASED BEFORE. NO ONE HAD EARLIER DETECTED THE ODOUR OF A DECOMPOSED BODY.

Pathologist Dr Chao Tzee Cheng performed the autopsy and came up with the following conclusions:

1.   The cause of death was due to a fractured cervical spine, and the fracture could have been due to:
  i.   A fall from a height. However, this would usually be accompanied by other external injuries.
  ii.   The head being snapped backwards by an external force.
  iii.   A blow by a blunt instrument to the front.
2.   The body was partially burnt.
3.   The clothes of the dead man were burnt at the back.
4.   Soot was found in the throat and air passages of the deceased. Since the body was already in a decomposed state when it was discovered, it could only mean that the soot had been inhaled in an earlier fire. The most unusual feature was that:
5.   The shirt pocket and inner trouser pockets of the deceased had been cut. Several one dollar notes and a ball-pen were found in the shirt pocket which had been cut vertically from the middle, and the trouser pockets cut horizontally near the bottom. The cutting of the pockets

could not have been done by the undertakers or morticians because decomposition had caused the body to swell and fit the trousers very tightly.

We have all the facts possible. Can we now, using these facts, picture roughly what MIGHT have happened?

The murderer might have been someone related to him, or someone he worked with, or worked for. We shall assume that that morning, Fong had gone to meet this person (or persons). Remember, Fong had been out to sea, and might have brought back something that someone else might have wanted. During their meeting, Fong and this person might not have seen eye to eye on the matter they were discussing. This person then grabbed a blunt object and hit Fong with it, or he was strong enough to fracture Fong's neck. The possibility of Fong falling and fracturing his cervical spine is not likely, because, like the pathologist had said, it would be accompanied by other external injuries. Fong, incapacitated by the blow, was still alive, but the assailant might have wanted to make it look as though the cause of death was through severe burns rather than a spine fracture.

According to Dr Chao, the pathologist, the body of the deceased was already decomposing when the firemen found him, yet there was soot in his throat and air passages, which could only mean that the victim inhaled the soot from another earlier fire. Therefore, the assailant might have tried to burn the victim, but not successfully, and later abandoned the idea. He might have hidden the body somewhere else for the next few days (since if he had dumped the body there, the odour would have attracted attention), and, when the opportunity arose, brought it to the lallang patch at Pepys Road where he could have started the fire; if not, a smouldering cigarette carelessly thrown on the grass that day, or even the heat of the sun, could have caused the grass to burn. But whether or not the body was brought there days before it was discovered, and whether or not the murderer started the fire or otherwise, it is evident that Fong was murdered.

The most puzzling circumstance of course, was the cutting of the pockets. But why? Could there have been something illegal, like drugs, sewn in the pockets? Or perhaps there was some incriminating evidence patterned or printed on the pockets that had to be removed because it pointed an accusing finger at someone, or some people?

* * * * * * * * * * * * * * * *

The cases are not solved. Could Lim Lian Choo and Fong Tee Kik have been murdered, and are their murderers (or even murderer) still on the loose?

Perhaps you could help.

BY THE SAME AUTHOR

PONTIANAK

"From parlour games gone fatally wrong, through monstrous school children, wicked practical jokes, murderous schizophrenia and with horrifying pontianaks in abundance, Nicky Moey has you screaming all the way ..."

—The Sunday Star

"The plots are deceptively simple, but neatly stop short of being predictable. The reader will be outguessed, and hugely pleased ..."

—The Straits Times

SONGS OF SUSPENSE

"Into the macabre aspect of these tales is woven an account of the touching frailties of human nature, the everpresent struggle between good and evil, so much so that the genre of the suspense story is given a new dimension ..."

—National Book Development Council of Singapore

"With his flair for the macabre and an obvious taste for the eerie, Moey has a delicate way of handling horror and dishing it out in a highly readable fashion ... He gets the readers worked up over the slightest tension."

—The Malay Mail